THE
REAL
CHRIST

We would see Jesus. (John 12:21)

*Then were the disciples glad, when
they saw the Lord.* (John 20:20)

The Christ of actual historical fact as distinguished from the Christ of man's dreams and fancies and imaginings: The Christ of God's own appointment whose picture God Himself has drawn in the Bible as distinguished from the Christ of Christian Science, theosophy, Unitarianism, spiritualism, and other forms of fiction.

Contents

Introduction

For years it has been on my heart to write a book on *the real Christ,* the Christ of actual historical fact as distinguished from the Christ of man's dreams and fancies and imaginings. I have spent many hours in the famous picture galleries of Europe, studying the paintings of "The Christ" by the so-called Masters, and I have always been disappointed and often indignant at the gross misrepresentations of the face of Jesus Christ as they presented it.

One night in a world-famous center of culture and art in the Old World, a man called to see me. As he entered the room and I glanced at his face, I felt confident that his face was the model of many of the supposed portraits of our Lord. With his opening sentence, he confirmed my suspicion. And why had he come to see me? Because he was the slave of sin in one of its most disgusting forms, and he came to discover if there was any way of deliverance. And the face of this moral degenerate was taken as a model by those who would portray the countenance of the perfect Man!

The representations of Christ by many poets, essayists, and preachers, while not so grossly false, nevertheless are not satisfying. They no more present *the real Christ* than Edwin

Arnold's *The Light of Asia* presented the real Buddha. But there is a perfect portrayal of *the real Christ,* the Christ of God's own appointment, the Christ of actual fact, in all His many-sided and complete perfection, beauty, and glory. That portrait is in God's own Word, the Bible. It is found in the preview of the coming Christ given to the Old Testament prophets, and in the histories of the Christ as He actually moved among men that the four evangelists in the New Testament were inspired by God to write. We also see it in the explanation of the picture that the apostles who wrote the epistles were enlightened by the Holy Spirit to give.

Over that marvelous picture I have pored for many days and weeks and months and years, and my wonder has grown as I have studied it. I attempted a number of years ago to give a series of addresses on *the real Christ* at a Bible conference. Not a few testified of being blessed, but I was not satisfied; I studied on and prayed that I might see Him and tell of Him as He actually was. At last I decided to attempt, by the Holy Spirit's enabling, to interpret God's own picture of the Christ of His own appointment and share it with my own people and then put the interpretation into book form for wider circulation.

My wife is somewhat responsible for the decision. She delights not only in an instructive rather than a merely persuasive ministry, but also in a ministry that is coherent, orderly, progressive, systematic, symmetrical, and complete in its teaching. So she said to me one day last October as we were crossing the Pacific Ocean to America from China, "What series of sermons are you going to preach on next winter?"

"I do not know."

"Well, you are going to preach a series of some kind, are you not?"

"I suppose so."

"Well, about what?" She was insistent and there was no escape.

"Perhaps about *the real Christ*."

"I think that would be a good subject."

I prayed, and a higher Authority confirmed, "Preach on *the real Christ*," and I did. I have never enjoyed preaching any other phase of God's truth as much as I have in presenting this. Sometimes I could hardly go on with my dictation as I have perceived His wondrous beauty; and repeatedly as I have spoken to the people and I have seen the Lord, a strange, glad awe has fallen upon speaker and hearers alike. And the crowds have grown; many have been blessed, and great changes have taken place in the preacher and in the hearers. May God bless the reading of these studies as He has the preaching and hearing of them.

Chapter 1

The Real Christ

And the Word was made flesh, and dwelt among us, (and we beheld his glory, the glory as of the only begotten of the Father,) full of grace and truth. (John 1:14)

But we all, with open face beholding as in a glass the glory of the Lord, are changed into the same image from glory to glory, even as by the Spirit of the Lord. (2 Corinthians 3:18)

He that saith he abideth in him ought himself also so to walk, even as he walked. (1 John 2:6)

Therefore let all the house of Israel know assuredly, that God hath made the same Jesus, whom ye have crucified, both Lord and Christ. (Acts 2:36)

My subject in this chapter is *the real Christ*, taken from a series of sermons on this subject. *He that saith he abideth in him ought himself also so to walk, even as he walked.* We hear a great deal about Christ in our day. It is doubtful if there was ever an age before this in which men talked and wrote so much about Christ as today. We hear about Christ not only from thoroughly orthodox, evangelical Christians, but we also hear about Christ from Roman Catholics. We hear about Christ from Unitarians. We hear about Christ from theosophists. We hear about Christ from Christian Scientists. We hear about Christ from spiritualists. We hear about Christ from some Buddhists. We hear about Christ from Behaists, and we hear about Christ from socialists and anarchists. We hear about Christ even from men and women who make no profession whatever of any religion of any sort. You see His name, His title, and His sign everywhere.

But the Christ many tell about and urge upon men is not the real Christ. He is not the actual Christ Jesus who once walked this earth and whom men saw and studied and knew – the Christ who was the incarnate Word of God and whose glory men actually saw with their own eyes, *the glory as of the only begotten of the Father, full of grace and truth.* He is not the Christ who once lived and died and was raised again. The Christ many talk about is a pure figment of their own imagination, which they have substituted for the actual Christ of history, the Christ who once lived here on earth and who now lives in glory. He will come back someday to take the reins of government and save this wrecked and ruined human society of ours; He will make it what it ought to be.

For example, the Christ of Christian Scientists is not the real Christ. You sometimes think when you hear Christian Scientists talk about Christ that they are talking about our Lord Jesus Christ, and that, as they say they believe in the divinity of Christ, they mean that they believe in the deity of Jesus. Not for one moment do they mean that. By *Christ* they do not mean a definite person at all, any more than they mean a definite person when they speak about God. They mean the "Christ principle."

The Christ of theosophy is not the real Christ. Even the Christ of Roman Catholicism is not the real Christ, even if in some measure He is. The Roman Catholics, when they speak about Christ, mean the Jesus who was crucified, has risen, and is coming again; they even mean a divine Jesus, but the picture they draw of Him, His character, and His relationship to His virgin mother, is very different from the picture God Himself has drawn in this Book. And the Christ pictured in many a Protestant pulpit is not the real Christ.

The only place to see the real Christ, just as He was and is, is in this Book. Today many say that they believe in Christ but not in the Christ of the Bible; but there is no other Christ than the Christ of the Bible. Any Christ other than the Christ of the Bible is a pure figment of the individual imagination, a mere idol substituted for a divine reality. Any Christ other than the biblical one is just as much an idol, though manufactured by man's brains, as an idol that men manufacture with their hands out of iron, silver, gold, wood, or stone.

Any Christ other than the Christ of the Bible is a pure figment of the individual imagination.

The real Christ is set forth in our first text: *And the Word was made flesh, and dwelt among us, (and we beheld his glory, the glory as of the only begotten of the Father,) full of grace and truth* (John 1:14). And He is set forth in our second text, Acts 2:36: *Let all the house of Israel therefore know assuredly, that God hath made him both Lord and Christ, this Jesus whom ye crucified.* That man Jesus who walked this earth two thousand years ago, who was God manifest in the flesh, He and He alone is the real Christ. And the whole Book tells about Him, not merely the four Gospels but also the entire sixty-six books

3

that make up the Bible, and in this chapter we will study Him as pictured in this Book.

I have said that the Bible is the only book that can help us to truly know Him, the real Christ. Let me add that the Holy Spirit is the only person who can enable us to understand Him as He is set forth in the Bible. God has drawn the picture of the real Christ in the Bible, and the Holy Spirit is God's interpreter of the picture. The work of the Holy Spirit is to bear witness of the real Christ (John 15:26); only as He testifies of Christ, as He takes the picture given to us in the written Word of God and interprets it for us, can we come to know and understand the real Christ, Jesus Christ.

We have a threefold objective in studying the real Christ:

1. That we may see Him in all His moral glory: *The glory as of the only begotten of the Father, full of grace and truth*, and we may therefore admire and love and glorify Him as we ought.

2. That we may become like Him when we see Him, or as the American Standard Version of 2 Corinthians 3:18 puts it: *We all, with unveiled face beholding as in a mirror the glory of the Lord, are transformed into the same image from glory to glory, even as from the Lord the Spirit.*

3. That in Him we may have a standard for our own conduct, or as John puts it in our third text: *He that saith he abideth in him ought himself also so to walk, even as he walked* (1 John 2:6). The Ten Commandments are not the Christian's rule of life. The Christian has a far higher rule of life than the Ten Commandments. Jesus Christ Himself is the Christian's rule of life. *He that saith he abideth in him ought himself also so to walk, even as he walked.*

Jesus Christ, the Holy One

We look at the Christ today in the most fundamental feature of His character. What do you think is the most fundamental attribute of the character of Jesus Christ? Holiness! We look at the Christ in this chapter as the Holy One. Holiness is the first and most preeminent characteristic of Jesus Christ that appears in the Word of God. As John puts it in our first text: *We beheld his glory, the glory as of the only begotten of the Father.* Now, holiness is the preeminent, moral characteristic of God, and it is, therefore, also the preeminent characteristic of Jesus Christ. It is true, John says in 1 John 4:8 that *God is love,* but John had previously mentioned something else. He had revealed the deeper foundation on which he could build the statement, *God is love,* and that deeper something is found in 1 John 1:5: *This then is the message which we have heard of him, and declare unto you, that God is light, and in him is no darkness at all.*

The whole object of the Old Testament revelation, which was to form the basis of the New Testament revelation, was to teach, enlighten, and burn into the Jewish consciousness one great fundamental truth, namely, God is holy. Holiness was the fundamental, preeminent, moral attribute of God, and it is the fundamental, preeminent, moral attribute of the real Christ. Christ was loving? Yes. Christ was gentle and merciful? Yes. Christ was meek and humble and prayerful? Yes. We shall study all these attributes of Christ in their place, but Christ was first of all holy. He, too, was *light, and in him [there was] no darkness at all* (1 John 1:5).

We shall divide the holiness of Christ into two categories: the fact of His holiness and how the holiness of Jesus Christ manifested itself.

The Fact of the Holiness of the Real Christ

We shall look first at the fact of the holiness of the real Christ, which is set forth in the Bible in many ways.

Repetition of His Holiness
The fact of Christ's holiness is clearly, directly, and definitely declared repeatedly. In Acts we read: *For of a truth against thy holy child Jesus, whom thou hast anointed, both Herod, and Pontius Pilate, with the Gentiles, and the people of Israel, were gathered together. By stretching forth thine hand to heal; and that signs and wonders may be done by the name of thy holy child Jesus* (Acts 4:27, 30). Here the holiness of Jesus is twice emphasized as the one completely descriptive moral attribute of Christ Jesus.

In Mark we read: *An unclean spirit . . . cried out, saying, Let us alone; what have we to do with thee, thou Jesus of Nazareth? art thou come to destroy us? I know thee who thou art, the Holy One of God* (Mark 1:23-24). Here a demon, a being of superior intelligence but inferior character, is compelled to declare the truth that Jesus was not only holy but that He was also *the Holy One of God.*

It is evident that Jesus Christ was absolutely holy, like the Jehovah of the Old Testament.

Again in Acts we read: *But ye denied the Holy One and the Just, and desired a murderer to be granted unto you* (Acts 3:14). Here the apostle Peter, filled with the Holy Spirit, declares Jesus to be *the Holy One.*

First John 2:20 says, *But ye have an unction from the Holy One, and ye know all things.* The *Holy One* here, as is evident from a careful study of the passage, is Jesus Christ, and again an inspired apostle declares Him to be the Holy One. Putting these passages together, it is evident that Jesus Christ was holy, absolutely holy, like the Jehovah of the Old Testament – the Holy One.

In the Old Testament, Jehovah God is called the Holy One. Consider the book of Isaiah alone, and we find that Isaiah declares Jehovah to be the Holy One of Israel no less than thirty times. But when the Christ appeared in the person of Jesus of Nazareth, when Jehovah became flesh and tabernacled in the person of Jesus Christ, it was He who was set forth as the Holy One. *Holy* means absolutely free from moral defilement or defect. To say that Jesus Christ is the Holy One, absolutely holy, is to say that Jesus Christ *is light, and in him is no darkness at all* (1 John 1:5). And Jesus Christ did not hesitate to say of Himself, *I am the light of the world: he that followeth me shall not walk in darkness, but shall have the light of life* (John 8:12).

Repetition of Words and Phrases
The fact that Jesus Christ was holy, absolutely holy, is brought out in the Bible by the way in which the Bible repeats words, phrases, and figures to produce an adequate impression of the absolute holiness or moral purity of Christ. For example, we read:

> *For such a high priest became us, holy, guileless, undefiled, separated from sinners, and made higher than the heavens* (Hebrews 7:26).

> *How much more shall the blood of Christ, who through the eternal Spirit offered himself without blemish unto God, cleanse your conscience from dead works to serve the living God?* (Hebrews 9:14).

> *But with the precious blood of Christ, as of a lamb without blemish and without spot* (1 Peter 1:19).

*And ye know that he was manifested to take away
our sins; and in him is no sin* (1 John 3:5).

*For he hath made him to be sin for us, who knew no
sin; that we might be made the righteousness of God
in him* (2 Corinthians 5:21).

*For we have not an high priest which cannot be
touched with the feeling of our infirmities; but was
in all points tempted like as we are, yet without sin*
(Hebrews 4:15).

*And every man that hath this hope in him purifieth
himself, even as he is pure* (1 John 3:3).

Note how the Holy Spirit through these various inspired men
piles up figures and phrases to produce in our minds something
like an adequate impression of the immaculate and absolute
and infinite holiness of Jesus Christ. Truly we do *[behold] his
glory, the glory as of the only begotten of the Father, full of grace
and truth.* The dazzling white light that transformed and glorified the face and very garments of Jesus on Mount Tabor was
only a faint image of the moral glory of His infinite holiness
that shone within. And yet many, in the face of all this, dare to
compare their own holiness with the holiness of Jesus Christ
and say that they have already attained unto all the fullness
there is in Him.

When I look at Him in His infinite holiness, I wish to do
what Isaiah did when he *saw also the* LORD . . . *high and lifted
up,* and heard the seraphim cry in His presence, *Holy, holy,
holy, is the* LORD *of hosts.* I wish to cover my face and cry, *Woe
is me! for I am undone; because I am a man of unclean lips, and
I dwell in the midst of a people of unclean lips* (Isaiah 6:1, 3, 5).

I cannot but do what Job did when he no longer merely heard of God by the hearing of the ear, but his eyes also saw Him: *I abhor myself, and repent in dust and ashes* (Job 42:6).

How the Holiness of Jesus Christ Manifests Itself

Now let us look at how the holiness of the real Christ, Jesus of Nazareth, manifested itself.

In a Love of Righteousness
First of all, the holiness of Jesus Christ manifested itself in a love of righteousness and a hatred of iniquity. We read in Hebrews 1:9: *Thou hast loved righteousness, and hated iniquity; therefore God, even thy God, hath anointed thee with the oil of gladness above thy fellows.* It is not enough to love righteousness; iniquity must be hated as well. On the other hand, it is not enough to hate iniquity; righteousness must be loved as well. Some profess to love righteousness, but they do not seem to hate iniquity. They are strong in applauding right but not equally strong in denouncing evil. Some also profess to hate sin, but they do not seem to love righteousness. They are strong in denouncing evil but not equally strong in applauding right. The holiness of the real Christ, our Lord Jesus, was complete as well as spotless – He loved righteousness and hated iniquity.

In Deed and Word
The holiness of Jesus Christ also manifested itself both in deed and word: negatively by His never sinning or speaking falsehood; positively by His always pleasing God and speaking the things that pleased God. For example:

9

*Who did no sin, neither was guile found in his
mouth* (1 Peter 2:22).

*And he that sent me is with me: the Father hath not
left me alone; for I do always those things that please
him* (John 8:29).

*While he yet spake, behold, a bright cloud over-
shadowed them: and behold a voice out of the cloud,
which said, This is my beloved Son, in whom I am
well pleased; hear ye him* (Matthew 17:5).

*For I have not spoken of myself; but the Father
which sent me, he gave me a commandment, what I
should say, and what I should speak* (John 12:49).

Note carefully two things. First, the holiness of Christ manifested itself not merely in His deeds but also in His words. Many
today who make great professions of holiness in their activities
are very unholy in their communication. Second, note that the
holiness of Christ did not merely manifest itself negatively in
not doing or speaking wrong but also positively in speaking and
doing all that God desired – all that was right to do or speak. A
full manifestation of holiness does not consist merely in doing
nothing wrong but also in doing all that is right and saying all
that ought to be said. It is comparatively easy never to say what
we ought not to say and never to do what we ought not to do,
but the really hard thing is to always do the thing God would
be pleased to have us do and always say the thing, everything,
God would have us say.

In Victory over Sin
The holiness of Christ was manifested in constant and never-failing

victory over sin. This is brought out in Hebrews 4:15: *For we have not an high priest which cannot be touched with the feeling of our infirmities; but was in all points tempted like as we are, yet without sin.* The holiness of our Lord was not the mere negative innocence that results from being shielded from contact with evil, but it was also the positive holiness that meets evil and overcomes it.

In His Uncompromising Standard

The holiness of Jesus Christ manifested itself in demanding absolute perfection in His disciples and refusing any compromise with evil. This comes out in Matthew 5:48: *Be ye therefore perfect, even as your Father which is in heaven is perfect.* The whole Sermon on the Mount is an illustration of this same thing. Because Jesus Christ was infinitely holy, He could not be satisfied with anything less in you and me than perfect holiness. Some say, "I wish He had set the standard lower," but I rejoice and glorify God that He set the standard as high as He did. If He had set the standard lower, He would not have been the real Christ, an absolutely holy Christ.

> **The holiness of our Lord was the positive holiness that meets evil and overcomes it.**

In His Rebuke of Sinners

In the fifth place, the holiness of Jesus Christ manifested itself in the stern and scathing rebuke of sinners. This we see repeatedly. For example: *But woe unto you, scribes and Pharisees, hypocrites! for ye shut up the kingdom of heaven against men: for ye neither go in yourselves, neither suffer ye them that are entering to go in* (Matthew 23:13). *But he turned, and said unto Peter, Get thee behind me, Satan: thou art an offence unto me: for thou savourest not the things that be of God, but those that be of men* (Matthew 16:23).

Jesus Christ disclosed the sin of the woman of Samaria in a similar unsparing way as we read: *The woman answered and said, I have no husband. Jesus said unto her, Thou hast well said, I have no husband: for thou hast had five husbands; and he whom thou now hast is not thy husband: in that saidst thou truly* (John 4:17-18).

Ye serpents, ye generation of vipers, how can ye escape the damnation of hell? (Matthew 23:33).

Why did our loving Lord rebuke sin so sternly, so scathingly, so mercilessly? Because He had to. Because of what He was. Because He was holy. Because He was *light, and in him [was] no darkness at all.* Oh yes, He was the meek and lowly Jesus, but not the meek and lowly Jesus as He is so often caricatured, looking on sin with indulgence and excuse and allowance. No, never! Repentant sinners He loved. Sin He hated and rebuked it sternly and scathingly with words that shriveled as a hot fire.

In His Sacrifice
In the sixth place, the holiness of our Lord Jesus Christ manifested itself in His making the greatest sacrifice in His power to save others from the sin He hated to the righteousness He loved. We are told this over and over again. For example: *Who his own self bare our sins in his own body on the tree, that we, being dead to sins, should live unto righteousness: by whose stripes ye were healed* (1 Peter 2:24). *For Christ also hath once suffered for sins, the just for the unjust, that he might bring us to God, being put to death in the flesh, but quickened by the Spirit* (1 Peter 3:18). *For he hath made him to be sin for us, who knew no sin; that we might be made the righteousness of God in him* (2 Corinthians 5:21).

We read again in a most remarkable passage in Philippians: *Who, existing in the form of God, counted not the being on an equality with God a thing to be grasped, but emptied himself, taking the form of a servant, being made in the likeness of men; and being found in fashion as a man, he humbled himself, becoming obedient even unto death, yea, the death of the cross* (Philippians 2:6-8).

The clear meaning of this is that in order to save men from the sin He hated to the righteousness He loved, He deliberately turned His back on equality with God, became a man, and submitted Himself to the lowest disgrace and the worst suffering a man could endure. Who can fathom such holiness as that?

Again in Galatians 3:13 we read: *Christ hath redeemed us from the curse of the law, being made a curse for us: for it is written, Cursed is every one that hangeth on a tree.* A wonderful statement of the same great truth is found in the Old Testament in Isaiah's prophetic vision of the coming Christ: *But he was wounded for our transgressions, he was bruised for our iniquities: the chastisement of our peace was upon him; and with his stripes we are healed. All we like sheep have gone astray; we have turned every one to his own way; and the* LORD *hath laid on him the iniquity of us all* (Isaiah 53:5-6).

Here was the crowning manifestation of the holiness of our Christ as He really was. He so hated sin and so loved righteousness that He was not only willing to die rather than to sin, but He was also willing to give up His divine glory and become a man. He was willing to die the death of a criminal, being rejected by man and separated from God, that others might not sin. He was willing to make any sacrifice to do away with sin, not in Himself but in others.

Men look at the cross of Christ and say, "See the love of God and the love of Christ." Yes, they are wonderfully set forth there, but look again at the cross of Jesus and see the holiness of Christ in His atoning death. He so hated sin and so loved righteousness that He made the matchless, marvelous, unfathomable sacrifice at the cross of shame in order to save not Himself, but other men and women from the sin He hated to the righteousness He loved.

In Future Punishment for Sin

The holiness of Jesus Christ will in the future manifest itself in the awful, irrevocable punishment of those who refuse to be separated from their sin. That is revealed repeatedly in the Scriptures. For example, we read those appalling words of our Lord: *When the Son of man shall come in his glory, and all the holy angels with him, then shall he sit upon the throne of his glory: and before him shall be gathered all nations: and he shall separate them one from another, as a shepherd divideth his sheep from the goats. Then shall he say also unto them on the left hand, Depart from me, ye cursed, into everlasting fire, prepared for the devil and his angels* (Matthew 25:31-32, 41).

The real Jesus is just as holy as God, and God is just as loving as Jesus.

Again we read in Thessalonians: *At the revelation of the Lord Jesus from heaven with the angels of his power in flaming fire, rendering vengeance to them that know not God, and to them that obey not the gospel of our Lord Jesus: who shall suffer punishment, even eternal destruction from the face of the Lord and from the glory of his might* (2 Thessalonians 1:7-9).

Why must men who will not forsake sin and receive the Savior perish forever? Because the real Christ is holy. He died to save men whom He loves from sin, which He hates. He stopped at no sacrifice to accomplish that. Language fails to describe the sacrifice He made.

But, if men themselves refuse to be separated from their sins, He leaves them to their self-chosen partnership and the doom which it involves. Men talk much of the holiness of God and the love of Jesus, but the real Jesus is just as holy as God, and God is just as loving as Jesus. In this and in everything else, Jesus and the Father are one.

Let us remember then, in trying to picture the real Christ, that the real Christ is first of all holy. Until we have an adequate perception of His holiness, we can have no adequate perception of His love.

In summary: *And the Word was made flesh, and dwelt among us, (and we beheld his glory, the glory as of the only begotten of the Father,) full of grace and truth* (John 1:14).

Chapter 2

The Real Christ:
His Love for the Father

Let all the house of Israel therefore know assur-
edly, that God hath made him both Lord and
Christ, this Jesus whom ye crucified. (Acts 2:36)

But that the world may know that I love the
Father, and as the Father gave me commandment,
even so I do. (John 14:31)

Our general subject in this chapter is the same as in the
last. The real Christ – the Christ of God's own appointment and of actual historical fact – is distinguished from
the Christ of man's dreams and fancies and imaginings, the
Christ whose picture God Himself has drawn in the Bible as
distinguished from the Christ of Christian Science, theosophy,
Unitarianism, and other forms of fiction.

In chapter 1 we looked at one special feature of the picture
God has drawn: the holiness of Christ, Christ as the absolute

and infinitely Holy One. In this chapter we take another feature of the picture: the love of Jesus Christ for God the Father.

In our second text, the Lord Jesus, the true and only Christ of God, tells us that the one thing He wished the world to know about Him was that He loved the Father. Let me quote it to you again: *But that the world may know that I love the Father; and as the Father gave me commandment, even so I do.* Usually when we speak of love, it is love for our fellow man, or *humanitarianism,* as we love to call it, that we think of. Modern thought is so exclusively occupied with man that it scarcely enters our minds that God should be the supreme object of our love, and that our obligation to love God is immeasurably greater than our obligation to love our fellow man. Most people echo the sentiment of the gifted poet who really exalted the one who was "a lover of his fellow man" above the one who loved God.

Our obligation to love God is immeasurably greater than our obligation to love our fellow man.

Our Lord Jesus loved His fellow man; He loved His fellow man as no other human being ever loved His fellow man. We shall consider that in the next chapter. But far deeper than His love for his fellow man, the very foundation of that love, and high above that love, was His love for God. The one thing above all others that He wished the world to know of Him was *that He loved God; He loved the Father.* So it should be with us.

It is indeed important that we love our fellow man. Love for our fellow man is the only solution to our social problems, industrial problems, political problems, and international problems. No external United Nations organization will ever set things straight. No external social adjustment of any kind will set things straight. No triumph of universal democracy will ever set things straight. Only love in the heart of the individual man for other men will give us the solution. If love ruled in the hearts of capitalists and laborers, in the hearts of Americans, Englishmen, Italians, Russians, Germans, Japanese, Chinese, and the rest, then all our social, industrial, and international problems would be settled in a few days. And they never will be really settled until love for our fellow man is triumphant in the individual heart.

No philosopher and no millions of philosophers can bring in universal justice, equality, and peace while selfishness rules in the hearts of men. But as important as love for man is, love for God is more fundamental and immeasurably more important. God is infinite, and man is finite; one of the simplest truths of mathematics is that no number of finites ever equals infinity. The whole mass of the human race put together, all those now living on the earth and all the billions who have lived in ages past, are as the *small dust of the balance* compared with the one infinite God. If we should render our full measure of love for the whole human race and fail to love the one infinite God as we ought, where we succeeded would be as nothing compared to where we failed. We shall see that it was because Jesus loved God the Father that He loved His fellow man, and we shall never love our fellow man in reality until we first love God. As John put it: *We love, because he first loved us* (1 John 4:19), and by believing in that love, we get to love God and so then love our fellow man. He also said, *Beloved, if God so loved us, we also ought to love one another* (1 John 4:11).

It is the love of Jesus Christ for the Father that we will consider and meditate on in this chapter.

How Did Jesus' Love for the Father Manifest Itself?

In Obedience
The love of our Lord Jesus for the Father first manifested itself when Jesus did what the Father commanded. This comes out in

our text: *But that the world may know that I love the Father; and as the Father gave me commandment, even so I do* (John 14:31).

The same thought is found in John 15:10: *If ye keep my commandments, ye shall abide in my love; even as I have kept my Father's commandments, and abide in his love.*

Because Christ Jesus loved the Father with a true and not a pretended love, loved Him *in deed and in truth* and not merely *in word and tongue,* His ear was ever listening eagerly for the slightest or the hardest commandment of God, and the moment He heard it, He did it. So will everyone do who really loves God. Many of us talk about loving God, but our ears are not constantly listening for His word, and even when we are forced to hear it, we are slow to obey it.

It was for the sole purpose, a glad and not reluctant purpose, of obeying God, of doing the Father's will, that Jesus turned His back on heaven's glory and came down to the shame and agony of earth. He said, *For I came down from heaven, not to do mine own will, but the will of him that sent me* (John 6:38). His love for the Father did not make Him hesitate to abandon the glory of heaven for the shame of earth, because that was the Father's will. We should stop here, ponder that, and lay our lives alongside His to see how they measure up to God's standard man, Jesus the Christ.

Having come into this world in obedience to the Father's will, His loving obedience faltered not at death, even the death of the cross. As Paul said, *And being found in fashion as a man, he humbled himself, becoming obedient even unto death, yea, the death of the cross* (Philippians 2:8).

Jesus Christ's death was voluntary on His part. Some tell us today that it was an unavoidable incident of His fidelity to duty, but God tells us in His Word that it was the purpose for which He came into this world and the goal toward which He deliberately walked. Jesus said, *Therefore doth the Father love me, because I lay down my life, that I may take it again. No one taketh it away from me, but I lay it down of myself. I have power to lay it down, and I have power to take it again* (John 10:17-18).

We read in Luke 9:51 of His last journey to Jerusalem where the cross awaited Him: *And it came to pass, when the time was come that he should be received up, he stedfastly set his face to go to Jerusalem.* But it was not only on that last journey that *he stedfastly set his face to go to Jerusalem,* but when He first took upon Himself the nature of man, He also had steadfastly set His face to go to Calvary. The Jews, as they stood beside the tomb of Lazarus and saw Jesus weeping, said, *Behold how he loved him!* (John 11:36). We stand beside the cross and behold Jesus bleeding, suffering, agonizing, and dying, and we cry, "Behold how He loved Him, God the Father."

In Keeping His Father's Word

In the second place, the love of Jesus Christ for the Father manifested itself in His keeping and guarding His Father's Word. We read this in His own words in John: *And ye have not known him: but I know him; and if I should say, I know him not, I shall be like unto you, a liar: but I know him, and keep his word* (John 8:55). The word translated *keep* means "to attend to carefully" or "to guard." To keep God's Word means more than to obey His commandments. A man may obey commandments without hearty love for them, but we guard that which we regard as a precious treasure. So our Lord Jesus regarded the words of God. The Father's Word was His most precious treasure. He guarded it as other men guard their gold and jewels. This esteem for His Father's Word was a peculiar mark of His love for the Father.

> To keep God's Word means more than to obey His commandments.

How many there are today who profess to love God but need to learn this lesson! They do not jealously guard and tenaciously hold fast to God's Word. They are quite willing to give up any part of it when the first slick talker, who claims to be an interpreter of the most recent scholarship, says, "It is not authentic and all scholars are agreed it must go." What is the fundamental difficulty with these men? A lack of a deep and genuine love for the Father, such as Christ Jesus had. If they had that love for the Father, they would keep God's Word. They would hold on to God's Word regardless of who was displeased. Note again these words of the real Christ: *And ye have not known him: but I know him; and if I should say, I know him not, I shall be like unto you, a liar: but I know him and keep his word.*

In Unwavering Submission

In the third place, the love of Jesus Christ for the Father was manifested in unwavering submission to the Father's will, even when it might require that from which His soul shrank in heartbreaking anguish. This comes out in our Lord's words: *And he went forward a little, and fell on his face, and prayed, saying, My Father, if it be possible, let this cup pass away from me: nevertheless, not as I will, but as thou wilt. Again a second time he went away, and prayed, saying, My Father, if this cannot pass away, except I drink it, thy will be done* (Matthew 26:39, 42).

No man who ever lived on this earth so recoiled from death as our Lord Jesus did, for no other man was as full of life as He was. He contemplated death with heartbreaking agony. In view of His coming death, His soul was *exceeding sorrowful, even unto death;* but though He thus recoiled from it, He faced it and would face it gladly if it was the Father's will, and He knew that it was. Can we follow our Lord and Christ here? We must be ready to do so, for He has said, *If any man would come after me, let him deny himself, and take up his cross, and follow me* (Matthew 16:24).

In Positive Delight

The love of Jesus Christ for the Father also manifested itself in positive delight in doing the Father's will. This is disclosed in Psalm 40:8: *I delight to do thy will, O my God; yea, thy law is within my heart.* The will of the Father in which the Christ delighted in this case, as the context clearly shows, was His own sacrificial death on the cross. So we see Jesus was not only submissive to the Father's will when it required the cross, but that He also positively delighted in it, simply because it was the Father's will. Do you love God like that? Do you love Him so that you positively delight in His will simply because it is His will, even though it means crucifixion for you? Here lies the secret of a blessedness and a joy that nothing can ever mar.

Even in His boyhood, Jesus' delight was in the Father's will. This appears in Luke 2:48-49. His mother who had sought Him for three days said to Him, *Son, why hast thou thus dealt with us? behold, thy father and I sought thee sorrowing.*

He replied, *How is it that ye sought me? Wist ye not that I must be about my Father's business?* The American Standard Version translates it as, *Knew ye not that I must be in my Father's house?* The literal translation would be, *Knew ye not that I must be in the things of my Father?* The meaning evidently is that even in His boyhood, Jesus realized that He must be occupied with *the things of God* and that His delight was *in the things of God* and in the will of God.

During the entire course of His earthly life, doing His Father's will was His very meat and drink, His sustenance, His satisfaction, and His joy. We have a striking illustration of this in the fourth chapter of John. Jesus had come with His disciples to the well of Samaria at six o'clock in the evening. He was weary, thirsty, and hungry. His disciples had gone into Sychar to secure food for Him. He was too tired to accompany them. As He sat there, tired and hungry, on the well, the woman of

Samaria appeared, and Jesus Christ began to talk with her in order that He could give her the Living Water, that He might lead her to accept Himself and thus receive the Holy Spirit.

While He was deeply occupied in this work, the disciples returned and found Him talking with the woman. The disciples said to Him as they offered Him food, *Rabbi, eat.*

But he said unto them, I have meat to eat that ye know not.

Then the disciples said one to another, *Hath any man brought him aught to eat?*

And Jesus said to them, *My meat is to do the will of him that sent me, and to accomplish his work* (John 4:31-34).

He had forgotten His hunger and His weariness in the joy of doing the Father's will and accomplishing the Father's work. As we have said, doing His Father's will was His very meat and drink, His sustenance, His satisfaction, His joy.

In Pleasing the Father

Fifth, the love of Jesus Christ for the Father manifested itself in His always doing the things which were pleasing to the Father. Remember what He said: *He that sent me is with me; he hath not left me alone; for I do always the things that are pleasing to him* (John 8:29). Jesus, the Christ of God, so loved the Father that He made it His objective to find out what pleased the Father and always did it. That is far more than obedience to explicit commandments. A son may do whatever a father bids him, but a more loyal and loving son will not wait to be bidden but will study to find out what is pleasing to his father and anticipate the expression of his will. To know what was pleasing to the Father was Jesus Christ's constant concern; to do these things that were pleasing to the Father was His unwavering practice.

There is a lesson here we all need to learn, and not only learn but also keep in mind. Many of us think that if we do the things God specifically commands us to do and leave undone the things that God specifically commands us not to do, then we have done all that love for God requires of us. Oh, not at all. Love requires more than that. If we really have the love of God in our hearts, it requires us to make it our earnest and constant study to know what pleases God. It compels us. And when we know it, we will do it without waiting to be told.

How it would simplify our lives and how many of our perplexing problems it would solve if we would only proceed on that principle. Shall I go to the theater; shall I play cards; shall I patronize the movies; shall I smoke; shall I do this, that, and the other thing? The answer to all these questions is found in asking yourself the question, Will it bring more joy to God for me to do these things than for me not to do them? If it brings joy to Him, I will do them. Or, will it bring more joy to God for me not to do these things than for me to do them? If not doing them brings joy to Him, then if I really love God, I will not do them. Is that the principle upon which you act in everything? No? Then you do not love God. Learn from the Christ to love Him today, and from this time on make it the principle of your life to find out what would please Him for you to do and then do it every time.

> **If we really have the love of God in our hearts, it requires us to make it our earnest study to know what pleases God.**

In Seeking the Father's Will

In the sixth place, the love of Jesus Christ for the Father manifested itself in His seeking the Father's will. This we see in John 5:30: *I can of myself do nothing: as I hear, I judge: and my judgment is righteous; because I seek not mine own will, but the will of him that sent me.* The word translated *seek* in this verse means "to seek in order to find." It is used in Matthew 13:45 of a man seeking pearls. The thought is that the accomplishment of His Father's will was the one objective of Jesus Christ's pursuit. As other men hunt for jewels, gold, or pleasure, position or honor, or the accomplishment of their own will, so our Lord Jesus sought for the accomplishment of His Father's will. What are you seeking? Money, pleasure, honor, position, or just the accomplishment of God's will?

By Accepting Testimony and Glory from the Father Alone

The love of the real Christ, Christ Jesus, for the Father manifested itself in His seeking and accepting testimony and glory only from the Father. This we learn in the Gospel of John when Jesus said, *But the witness which I receive is not from man: howbeit I say these things, that ye may be saved. I receive not glory from men* (John 5:34, 41). Jesus Christ so loved the Father; the Father was so utterly everything to Him that He sought no praise and accepted no praise from man. It was the Father's testimony, the Father's approval, the Father's praise, and those things alone that He desired and would accept.

What a lesson for you and me. How eagerly and persistently we seek a little admiration and praise from men. How gladly we accept it when it comes. How we treasure the fine things that are said about us in newspapers or books. Let's stop it! Let us so utterly love God that His approval is all we care for and all we will accept.

By Finishing the Father's Work

In the eighth place, the love of Jesus Christ for the Father manifested itself in His finishing the work the Father gave Him to do. You will see this by reading John 17:4: *I have glorified thee on the earth: I have finished the work which thou gavest me to do.*

Jesus Christ loved the Father; therefore, He had to bring to a completion the work the Father assigned to Him. And when was that work completed? On the cross when He cried, *It is finished* (John 19:30). Then and not until then was the work completed.

Jesus recoiled from the cross in unutterable agony, but onward to the cross He marched because there, and there alone, the work the Father had given Him to do could be accomplished and completed. It was love for God the Father before love for you and me that brought our Lord Jesus to Calvary. We speak of God the Father loving men in Christ Jesus, which is true, but it is also true that Christ's sacrifice for men finds its final reason and original source in obedience to the will of the Father, who was the object of His supreme love.

Has God given you some work to do? He has – to each one of us. And does the completion of that work, the perfect consummation of it, lead to some Gethsemane or Calvary? Very likely. Let's march then to our Calvary, never hesitating a moment no matter how the heart recoils from the agony that awaits us there.

In Seeking Only the Glory of the Father
Finally, the love of Jesus Christ for the Father manifested itself in His seeking only the glory of the Father. This is revealed repeatedly in John: *I have glorified thee on the earth* (John 17:4). *He that speaketh of himself seeketh his own glory: but he that seeketh his glory that sent him, the same is true, and no unrighteousness is in him* (John 7:18). *These words spake Jesus, and lifted up his eyes to heaven, and said, Father, the hour is come; glorify thy Son, that thy Son also may glorify thee* (John 17:1).

> The Father's glory was Jesus Christ's first and great ambition, the consuming passion of His life.

The Father's glory was Jesus Christ's first and great ambition, the consuming passion of His life. It was for the Father's glory that He planned, prayed, lived, acted, suffered, and died. Jesus taught that the first and great commandment is: *Thou shalt love the Lord thy God with all thy heart, and with all thy soul, and with all thy mind* (Matthew 22:37). His own life is the supreme manifestation of this law which He taught. Is God's glory the only thing you are seeking? Have you lost sight utterly of your own glory, your own profit, your own ease, your own pleasure, your own everything? That is what Jesus, the Christ of God, did. And, *He that saith he abideth in him ought himself also to walk even as he walked* (1 John 2:6).

Chapter 3

The Real Christ:
His Love for Men

Let all the house of Israel therefore know assuredly, that God hath made him both Lord and Christ, this Jesus whom ye crucified. (Acts 2:36)

Unto him that loveth us, and loosed us from our sins by his blood. (Revelation 1:5)

For ye know the grace of our Lord Jesus Christ, that, though he was rich, yet for your sakes he became poor, that ye through his poverty might become rich. (2 Corinthians 8:9)

He that saith he abideth in him ought himself also so to walk, even as he walked. (1 John 2:6)

A new commandment I give unto you, That ye love one another; even as I have loved you, that ye also love one another. By this shall all men know that ye are my disciples, if ye have love one to another. (John 13:34-35)

Our subject in the first two chapters was the real Christ, the Christ of God's own appointment and actual historical fact, as distinguished from the Christ of man's dreams and fancies and imaginings. The real Christ is the Christ whose picture God Himself has drawn in the Bible as distinguished from the Christ of Christian Science, theosophy, Unitarianism, spiritualism, and other forms of fiction. We have the same general subject in this chapter. In the first chapter, however, we considered one feature of the picture of the real Christ which God has given in His Word: the holiness of the real Christ. In chapter 2 we considered a second feature of that picture: the love of Jesus Christ for the Father. Now we consider a third feature of the picture: the love of the real Christ, the Christ of God's own appointment, the Lord Jesus Christ, God manifest in the flesh, for His fellow man.

We have five wonderful texts; they have long meant much to us all, but before we finish this chapter I think they will mean more to some of us than they have ever meant before. We have already seen that our Lord Jesus loved His fellow man as no other man ever loved his fellow man; but far deeper than that love, the very foundation upon which His love rested and far higher than that love, was His love for God the Father. That is as it should be with us – our love for God the Father should be deeper, far deeper, and far higher than our love for our fellow man. Indeed, it must be the foundation of any real love for our fellow man.

But notwithstanding this, we shall see that the love of the real Christ for His fellow man was most amazing. And yet God tells us in His Word that in this love, Jesus, the Christ of God, set us an example that we should follow in His steps. As John said, *Hereby know we love, because he laid down his life for us: and we ought to lay down our lives for the brethren* (1 John 3:16).

What we have discovered in the picture God gives us in

His Word of the love of Christ for His fellow man will come under two headings:

First: Who among men Jesus Christ loved.

Second: How the love of the Christ for men manifested itself.

The Men Jesus Christ Loved

The Church

First of all, Jesus Christ loved the church. We find this explicitly stated in Ephesians 5:25: *Husbands, love your wives, even as Christ also loved the church, and gave himself up for it.* Jesus Christ, as we shall see later, loves all men, but the church is a special object of His love. The church is loved by Christ in a particular sense and in a special way. A philanthropist may love all mankind, and yet, if he is a true man, he will love his own wife in a special way

Christ has special love for the church, His bride.

as he loves no other woman. Likewise, Christ has special love for the church, His bride. We must be on our guard in studying the various passages in the Bible which speak about the love of Christ, to note whether they refer to His love in general for all mankind or His love in particular for the church, which is His body and His bride.

Who is meant by *the church*? Not, of course, any particular denomination and not the church as an external organization. By *the church* as used here and frequently in the New Testament, it means all the "called-out" of the present dispensation. In other words, it means all those who in this present dispensation accept Jesus Christ as their personal Savior, surrender to Him as their Lord and Master, confess Him as such before the world, and live a life of obedience to His will.

Christ's special love for the church is set forth in another way and a most beautiful way in John 13:1: *Now before the feast of the passover, Jesus knowing that his hour was come that he should depart out of this world unto the Father, having loved his own that were in the world, he loved them unto the end.* Here a body of people are spoken of as being *his own.* Of course, these are the same as the church. The reason they are called *his own* is made clear in John 17: *Even as thou gavest him authority over all flesh, that to all whom thou hast given him, he shall give eternal life. I pray for them: I pray not for the world, but for those whom thou hast given me; for they are thine. While I was with them, I kept them in thy name which thou hast given me: and I guarded them, and not one of them perished, but the son of perdition; that the scripture might be fulfilled* (John 17:2, 9, 12).

From these verses it is evident that Jesus Christ's *own* are those whom God the Father has given unto Him. There is a body of people out of the human race whom God has given unto Jesus Christ as His own special property; they are the ones who *received him* and *believeth on him* (John 1:12; 3:18). The proof that one belongs to this elect company is that he comes to Christ, as we read in John 6:37: *All that which the Father giveth me shall come unto me; and him that cometh to me I will in no wise cast out.* This highly favored company, given to Christ by the Father, comes to Christ; they are objects of Christ's special love. To them He ministers in a special way (John 13:1) and guards them so that not one of them perishes (John 17:12). Of them He says, *Of those whom thou hast given me I lost not one* (John 18:9).

Individual Believers

Jesus Christ not only loves the church as a body, He also loves individual believers in a particular way. That is evident in many Scriptures, but it comes out in a beautiful way in the words of Paul: *I have been crucified with Christ; and it is no longer I that live, but Christ liveth in me: and that life which I now live in the flesh I live in faith, the faith which is in the Son of God, who loved me, and gave himself for me* (Galatians 2:20).

Obedient Believers Who Loved Him

Jesus Christ loved with a particular love those who loved Him and showed their love by keeping His commandments. We read this in His own words: *He that hath my commandments, and keepeth them, he it is that loveth me: and he that loveth me shall be loved of my Father, and I will love him, and will manifest myself unto him* (John 14:21).

Our Lord Jesus expresses much the same thought in Mark 3:35: *For whosoever shall do the will of God, the same is my brother, and sister, and mother.* Whoever does the will of God stands in a relationship of the closest kinship to Christ; such a one is like His *brother, and sister, and mother.* A man may love all men and still have a special love for his own brother and sister and above all for his own mother, but our Lord tells us that He has that love which combines all three of these great loves for whoever does the will of God.

Special Individuals

Jesus loved special individuals in a special way. This appears in John 19:26 where John is spoken of as *the disciple . . . whom [Jesus] loved.* It also appears in John 11:5 where we are told that *Jesus loved Martha, and her sister, and Lazarus.* Yes, Jesus loves all men with infinite love; He has a special love for His church as His body and His bride; He has an individual love for each member of His body; He has a special love for those who have His commandments and keep them. But the more open any heart is to Him by faith and love, the more that person is the object of His special delight.

Sinners

Jesus Christ loved sinners – the lost, the ungodly, and the utterly vile. We see this repeatedly in the picture God has drawn of Him in the Bible. For example: *I came not to call the righteous, but sinners* (Matthew 9:13). *The Son of man came to seek and to save that which was lost* (Luke 19:10). *For while we were yet weak, in due season Christ died for the ungodly. But God commendeth his own love toward us, in that, while we were yet sinners, Christ died for us* (Romans 5:6, 8).

Christ pities the sinner. He delights in the saint. He loves them both. Jesus Christ loves the vilest sinner as truly as He loves the purest saint, but He does not love the vilest sinner in the same way He loves the purest saint. His love for the sinner is one thing; His love for the obedient disciple is quite another. Toward the one, He has pity; in the other, He takes pleasure. There is an attraction in both cases. In the one case, the attraction of need appeals to compassion; in the other case, the attraction of moral beauty appeals to appreciation and delight. Christ pities the sinner. He delights in the saint. He loves them both. In the parable of the lost sheep, we see that the attraction of need was greater than the attraction of moral beauty to Jesus (Luke 15:3-7).

Among the sinners whom Jesus loved were even His bitterest and cruelest enemies. We see Him on the cross forgetting His own dying agonies in His concern for those who nailed Him to the cross as He cries in His last moments, *Father, forgive them; for they know not what they do* (Luke 23:34). This is a lesson we all greatly need to learn from our Lord's example.

How the Love of Jesus Christ for Men Manifested Itself

We will now look at the picture God has drawn of the real

Christ in the Bible and see how His love for men manifested itself. I am staggered at the wealth of material that God gives us in His Word. I found there were no less than thirty separate and distinct ways in which the love of Jesus Christ for men manifested itself. Of course, it is impossible to give all of them in this chapter. Indeed, we must omit two-thirds of them. Which shall we select?

By Becoming Poor

In the first place, the love of Jesus Christ for men manifested itself in His becoming poor that we might become rich. This is seen in the following text: *For ye know the grace of our Lord Jesus Christ, that, though he was rich, yet for your sakes he became poor, that ye through his poverty might become rich* (2 Corinthians 8:9).

How great the riches He renounced and how great the poverty He assumed is seen in Philippians 2:6-8: *Who, existing in the form of God, counted not the being on an equality with God a thing to be grasped, but emptied himself, taking the form of a servant, being made in the likeness of men; and being found in fashion as a man, he humbled himself, becoming obedient even unto death, yea, the death of the cross.*

We see how great are the riches we obtain from His becoming so poor in Romans 8:16-17: *The Spirit himself beareth witness with our spirit, that we are children of God: and if children, then heirs; heirs of God, and joint-heirs with Christ.*

We might stop here, ponder and wonder, admire and adore our wondrous Lord, but we must move on. But before we do, even in this He has left us an example for our imitation: *He that saith he abideth in him ought himself also to walk even as he walked* (1 John 2:6).

By Giving Himself

The love of Jesus Christ for men manifested itself by His giving Himself up for us. We see this in a passage already quoted, Galatians 2:20: *The Son of God, who loved me, and gave himself up for me.* His was a self-sacrificing love; it was a love that sacrificed self, not merely His life for us. He sacrificed Himself for us. He *gave himself up* for us. The death of Christ was not the only sacrifice He made, though it was the crowning one. His whole life was a sacrifice from the manger to the cross. His becoming man at all was a sacrifice of immeasurable greatness and meaning.

Even in the marvelous sacrifice of Himself, we must follow in His steps. God tells us in Ephesians 5:2: *Walk in love, even as Christ also loved you, and gave himself up for us.* And God also says in words which can neither be misunderstood nor evaded: *Hereby know we love, because he laid down his life for us: and we ought to lay down our lives for the brethren* (1 John 3:16).

By Forgiving

The love of Jesus Christ for the vilest sinners manifested itself in His forgiving them when they repented of their sin and believed on Him. God's picture of the Christ abounds in illustrations of this. A notable instance is found in the seventh chapter of Luke. A woman who was a notorious sinner entered the house where He was being entertained by Simon the Pharisee.

She drew near to Him as He reclined at the table and, bending over His feet, wet them with her tears and wiped them with her hair. Simon and the other guests were shocked that He would allow a woman of such a character even to touch Him. But Jesus looked up into those tear-dimmed eyes and said, *Thy sins are forgiven. . . . Thy faith hath saved thee; go in peace* (Luke 7:48, 50). We are specifically told to imitate Him when others wrong us, for God says in Ephesians 4:32: *Be ye kind one to another, tenderhearted, forgiving each other, even as God also in Christ forgave you.*

By Rebuking and Chastening

The love of Jesus Christ for men manifested itself by His rebuking and chastening them when they sinned, to bring them to repentance. Speaking from glory, Jesus Christ said, *As many as I love, I reprove and chasten: be zealous therefore, and repent* (Revelation 3:19). A one-sided picture is often drawn of our Lord, the Christ of God, at this point. His readiness to forgive sinners, even the vilest, is emphasized, but that true and wise love of His that makes the impenitent sinner suffer so that he may be brought to repentance is lost sight of or obscured. Such a Christ is not the real Christ. It is not the Christ of actual fact. It is not the Christ God has pictured for us in His own Book.

By Patient Treatment

The love of Christ toward skeptics was manifested in His patient dealing with unreasonable, inexcusable, and stubborn doubts. There are various illustrations of this in the Bible. One of the most striking is in the case of Thomas. Thomas was not with the other disciples on the night of the resurrection day when Jesus appeared in their midst and manifested Himself to them. When Thomas returned, the other disciples said unto him, *We have seen the Lord,* but Thomas stubbornly replied, *Except I shall see in his hands the print of the nails, and put my finger into the print of the nails, and put my hand into his side, I will not believe* (John 20:24-25).

A week from that night, the next Lord's Day, the disciples were gathered again and Thomas was with them this time. Jesus stood in their midst and said, *Peace be unto you.* Then He turned to Thomas, the stubborn doubter, and gently said, *Thomas, Reach hither thy finger, and see my hands; and reach hither thy hand, and put it into my side: and be not faithless but believing.* The stubborn, unreasonable, inexcusable doubt of Thomas is conquered, and he falls upon his knees before his Lord, looks up into His face, and cries, *My Lord and my God* (John 20:26-28). There is a lesson for us here. We grow so impatient with the doubter, especially when he is stubborn and unreasonable in his doubt, but our Lord did not, and our Lord's method certainly is best.

By Tender Dealing with Backsliders

The love of Jesus Christ toward a weak disciple manifested itself by patient and tender dealing with his lapse into grievous sin and awful apostasy. The example that comes to mind is that of the apostle Peter who had denied his Lord three times with oaths and curses. But after His resurrection, our Lord sent a message through His angelic messengers to the disciples: *But go, tell his disciples and Peter, He goeth before you into Galilee: there shall ye see him, as he said unto you* (Mark 16:7).

When professing Christians prove weak, we are too ready to turn on them harshly and utterly discourage them.

Oh, how wondrously tender was that: *and Peter.* Why say, *and Peter?* Was he not a disciple? Yes, he was the leader of the apostolic company. But three nights prior to this, he had denied his Lord three times with oaths and curses; if the messenger had only said, "Tell His disciples," Peter would have said, "Yes, I was a disciple, but I am no longer. I denied my Lord with oaths and curses. He doesn't mean me." But our loving Lord sent the message: "Go and tell My disciples and, whoever you tell, be sure you tell poor, discouraged, backslidden, brokenhearted Peter."

Here too is a lesson for us. When professing Christians prove weak, when in the hour of testing they fail, we are too ready to turn on them harshly and utterly discourage them, instead of following in the footsteps of our Lord and dealing with them patiently and tenderly. No matter how grievous their lapse into sin may have been, we need to be patient and win them back to Him.

By Performing Menial Tasks
The love of Christ for His disciples manifested itself in His performing the lowliest and most menial services for them. We see this in that wonderful picture of the Christ that God has given us in John 13:1-5:

> *Now before the feast of the Passover, Jesus knowing*
> *that his hour was come that he should depart out*
> *of this world unto the Father, having loved his own*
> *that were in the world, he loved them unto the end.*
> *And during supper, the devil having already put into*
> *the heart of Judas Iscariot, Simon's son, to betray*
> *him, Jesus, knowing that the Father had given all*
> *things into his hands, and that he came forth from*
> *God, and goeth unto God, riseth from supper, and*
> *layeth aside his garments; and he took a towel,*
> *and girded himself. Then he poureth water into the*
> *basin, and began to wash the disciples' feet, and to*
> *wipe them with the towel wherewith he was girded.*

What a sight! What a sight! The Lord of glory washing the dirty feet of those mutually jealous disciples. But we cannot stop now to dwell on the significance of this wonderful scene. Indeed, what Jesus did on this occasion needs imitation more than it needs comment, and in this case our Lord definitely tells us and emphasizes the fact that He has left us an example that we should follow in His steps. His words are: *For I have given you an example, that ye also should do as I have done to you* (John 13:15).

By Leaving His Father

The love of Jesus Christ for the church was manifested in His leaving the Father to cleave unto the church, so that they too should become one flesh. This stupendous fact is declared by Paul: *For this cause shall a man leave his father and mother, and shall cleave to his wife; and the two shall become one flesh. This mystery is great: but I speak in regard of Christ and of the church* (Ephesians 5:31-32).

One hesitates to attempt to interpret these remarkable words, but God has put them into His Word that we may understand them and meditate upon them. Their meaning is plain, and it is staggering in its marvelous significance.

They mean this: God the Father was the object of the eternal love of Christ. In the eternity behind us, before a world or an angel or any created being was formed, God the Father and God the Son loved one another. Their whole being was wrapped up in one another. The tendrils of the love of Christ have wrapped themselves around the one object of His eternal love, the Father, with an infinitude of love that we cannot fathom or imagine. But man was created and man sinned; out of that great lost mass of mankind, God gave His Son a people who believed in Him and became His bride. Out of love for this bride, the eternal Son of God tore Himself away from the Father and came down to this sin-cursed world to win us as His bride and be joined to us. Do you wonder that Paul says, *This mystery is great?*

By Preparing a Place for Us

The love of Jesus Christ for His disciples manifested itself in His going to prepare a place for us. We see this in those familiar and precious words of our Lord: *In my Father's house are many mansions; if it were not so, I would have told you; for I go to prepare a place for you* (John 14:2). His love for the church brought Christ down to the earth, and His love for the church took Him away from the earth. His love for the church compelled Him to leave the Father to seek us out, win us for Himself as His bride, and die to secure our pardon. His love for the church also led him to go back to the Father and prepare an eternal home for us in His Father's house.

By His Coming Again

The love of Jesus Christ for His church will manifest itself in His coming again for us to receive us unto Himself, that we may be no more separated one from the other. This appears in the next verse to the one just quoted in John: *And if I go and prepare a place for you, I will come again, and receive you unto myself; that where I am, there ye may be also* (John 14:3). Oh, how He loves us! He left us out of love for us. He left us for our good. But He is lonesome without us; even heaven, with the Father's presence, is a lonesome place for Christ without us; He so loves us. And earth ought to be a lonesome place for us without our Lord and Christ, our heavenly Bridegroom, because we so love Him.

> Earth ought to be a lonesome place for us without our Lord and Christ.

Earth ought to be a lonesome place for us without Him no matter how beautiful our homes, how many our comforts, how numerous and excellent our friends, how noble and satisfying our children, our wives, or husbands. Is earth a lonesome place for you without the Lord Jesus? Are you longing for His return? Does your heart keep crying, *Even so, come, Lord Jesus,* come quickly (Revelation 22:20), and are you even willing, if He must tarry, to lay aside your mortal body and *be absent from the body, and to be at home with the Lord* (2 Corinthians 5:8)? Are you saying from the depths of your heart with Paul: "For me it would be far better to depart and be with Christ"?

There is a wonderful tenderness in the exact wording of this John 14:3 verse. Our Lord Jesus says, *I will come again, and receive you unto myself.* Note those words, *unto myself;* He does not merely say "into My home and into companionship with Me," but *unto myself.* It is as if He longed to press us to His very soul – *unto myself.* Frédéric Godet's comment on these words is worth repeating: "He presses him [the believer] to His heart, so to speak, while bearing Him away. There is an infinite tenderness in these last words. It is for Himself that He seems to rejoice in and look to this moment, which will put an end to all separation."

Last summer I entered a room in a little mission station in China, many miles off the beaten path. The native pastor dwelt in this room. There was just one decoration on the wall of that plainly furnished room – a text of Scripture. What do you think it was? Just these words: "Come quickly, Lord Jesus."

Chapter 4

The Real Christ:
His Love for Souls

Let all the house of Israel therefore know assuredly,
that God hath made him both Lord and Christ,
this Jesus whom ye crucified. (Acts 2:36)

For the Son of man came to seek and to save that
which was lost. (Luke 19:10)

And the multitude cometh together again, so that
they could not so much as eat bread. And when his
friends heard it, they went out to lay hold on him:
for they said, He is beside himself. (Mark 3:20-21)

And when he cometh home, he calleth together
his friends and his neighbors, saying unto them,
Rejoice with me, for I have found my sheep which
was lost. (Luke 15:6)

O Jerusalem, Jerusalem, that killeth the prophets,
and stoneth them that are sent unto her! how often
would I have gathered thy children together, even
as a hen gathereth her chickens under her wings,
and ye would not! (Matthew 23:37)

He that saith he abideth in him ought himself also
to walk even as he walked. (1 John 2:6)

For three chapters we have been studying, under the Holy Spirit's guidance, the picture God has given in His own Word, the Bible, of the real Christ. We've seen the Christ He has appointed, the Christ of actual historical fact as distinguished from the Christ of man's own manufacture, the Christ of man's fancy and imagination and dreams, and the Christ of Christian Science, theosophy, Unitarianism, spiritualism, and other forms of religious or irreligious fiction. We have thus far studied three features of that picture: first, the holiness of the real Christ; second, His love for God the Father; third, His love for men. Now we study the fourth feature of that divinely drawn picture – the love of Jesus Christ for souls. I have listed the above six texts for this purpose.

We shall study the Bible together to discover how the love of Jesus Christ for souls is seen, hoping that this study will awaken in us the same love for souls. Oh, how I wish it would; how much it would mean for this city, for this whole country, and for the world.

His Purpose for Coming

The love of Jesus Christ for souls is seen in the purpose for which He came into this world. He declared that purpose in Luke 19:10: *For the Son of man came to seek and to save that which was lost.* Seeking and saving the lost was the one great objective of the earthly mission of the Son of God. He came into this world not to receive honor, accumulate wealth, or gain a kingdom. He left behind greater glories than this world contained. He came for just one purpose – to seek out and save the lost.

Lost men were of more value and preciousness in His sight than all earth's wealth and glory. Yes, more than all the wealth and glory of the wonderful heaven He left behind. Indeed, in His sight a single soul was of priceless value. In His sight, the whole material universe did not have the value of a single soul – not merely the soul of someone great or wise or good, but also the soul of the most insignificant person. He valued the soul of the most foolish and unlearned, the soul of the vilest and the worst, not only the soul of the philosopher or the saint; He valued the soul of the savage and the outcast. Each soul has this value in His sight.

Years ago one Sunday night, I walked up the Waterloo Road in London. The street was a blaze of light. The taverns were in full blast. Stages were crowded with men and women, many of whom were drunk. I came to a dark place in the road. I saw a donkey cart backed up against the curb. Two young men were casting what looked like a filthy, stuffed bag into the donkey cart. I stepped nearer to see just what they were throwing into the cart. It was a woman, intoxicated and unconscious with drink, a woman perhaps fifty years old, seemingly their mother. I shrank back in horror and disgust, and then the thought came to me: *God loves that woman as truly as He loves you.* Not only is that true, but it is also true that in the sight of Jesus Christ, the soul of a poor, disgusting, intoxicated, degraded creature like that is of more value than all the priceless gems of earth. He *came to seek and to save that which was lost.*

Some years later, as I went through the streets of Benares, India, I saw a *fakir,* a so-called holy man, in a cage, almost naked, sitting before a fire. He stared at the fire and tried not to even wink his eyes or notice the people gazing at him. His hair

> **In His sight, the whole material universe did not have the value of a single soul.**

and his body were covered with ashes, a perfect representative of the Buddhist concept of holiness and blessedness. It was a more nauseating sight than the degraded, drunken woman in London, and again, as I turned away in disgust, the thought came to me: *God loves that poor, wretched being, blinded and sunken through the influence of Buddhism.* Yes, that is true, but it is also true that the soul of that poor, misguided, ignorant, degraded Buddhist *fakir* was of more value in the sight of Jesus Christ, and of those who see as Jesus Christ sees, than all the wealth and splendor of this world.

Jesus Christ, the eternal Word of God, left heaven and all its glory and came down to earth with all its pain, agony, and shame to seek out and save such people. He came to seek and to save the lost so that *though he was rich, yet for your sakes he became poor, that ye through his poverty might become rich* (2 Corinthians 8:9). He left His glory to seek and to save the lost: *Who, existing in the form of God, counted not the being on an equality with God a thing to be grasped, but emptied himself, taking the form of a servant, being made in the likeness of men; and being found in fashion as a man, he humbled himself, becoming obedient even unto death, yea, the death of the cross* (Philippians 2:6-8).

Do we have that love for souls that we would be willing to give up the highest place of earth's honor and take the lowliest place? Are we willing to take the place of misunderstanding, rejection, shame, spitting, suffering, and death to find more of the lost, the degraded, and the degenerate, and save them by leading them to know our Lord and Savior Jesus Christ?

His Continual Watchfulness for Souls

We see the love of Jesus Christ for souls in His always being on the watch for opportunities to save perishing souls. We have a striking illustration of this in the fourth chapter of John. You know the story. Jesus came to Jacob's well at six o'clock in the evening after a long day's journey. He was hungry and tired. His disciples went into the city to obtain food, but He was too tired to go with them, and as He sat there on the well, He lifted His eyes and saw a woman who was an outcast coming toward Him.

Immediately He forgot His hunger and His weariness. It was an opportunity such as He always longed for and watched for, an opportunity to tell a lost one the way of life. The moment she came within speaking distance, He opened a conversation with her by asking her for a drink of water, not so much that His own thirst might be quenched, but to gain an opening to tell her of the way of life and the Living Water – of which if one drinks, he shall never thirst.

We have another illustration in the ninth chapter of John where Jesus went and found the blind man whom He had healed but whom the Jews had cast out of the synagogue. He said to him, *Dost thou believe on the Son of God?* and then revealed Himself to him as the Son of God (John 9:35).

We see still another illustration in the second chapter of Mark where the determined four men brought their paralyzed friend to Jesus for healing. When they could not get through the door, they went up on the roof, broke open the tiles, and let their needy friend down right before Jesus. Instantly Jesus saw not only a paralyzed body to be healed but also a lost soul to be saved, and before He told him to arise and take up his bed and walk, He said to him, *Son, thy sins are forgiven* (Mark 2:5). Stalker said in his *Imago Christi* that Jesus Christ "made use of His miracles as stepping-stones to reach the soul." So should we use every act of kindness that God gives us as an opportunity and an opening for reaching the soul of the one for whom we perform it. But we should also always be on the alert for opportunities to save the lost.

Sometime ago, Rufus Smith, a quaint man of God, went up and down the eastern part of this country. He was a man on fire with a passion for the salvation of the lost. I first met him when he was an old man. It was my privilege once to travel with him from Washington to Atlanta. At every station, he would step out of the train and talk to the men on the platform. Afterward he came to visit me in Minneapolis. He was vulnerable to pneumonia but insisted on coming to the mission and speaking. After the mission meeting was over, someone spoke to him about the illumination of the principal business street in Minneapolis. It was only a few blocks away, and he insisted on going to see it. He would listen to no warning or protest. He was wrapped well in a heavy overcoat.

When we reached Nicollet Avenue, there was a blaze of light from the electric arches, and he saw a great crowd surging down the sidewalk and filling the roadway. He became very excited. He turned to me and said, "I can't stand this, I must preach." He tore off his overcoat and, handing it to me, stepped out into the middle of the street and lifted his voice: "Friends, I never saw anything like this. I am from Missouri. We never have anything like this down there. This is wonderful." The crowd stopped and gathered around him; they thought he was some greenhorn from the country and that there was some fun brewing.

His voice rang out again: "I never saw anything like this. This is wonderful." He stopped a moment and then said with intense earnestness, "But this is nothing to what soon shall be: *they that be wise shall shine as the brightness of the firmament; and they that turn many to righteousness as the stars for ever and ever*" (Daniel 12:3), and then he poured out his soul in a gospel message.

His Going after Lost Souls

Jesus Christ's love for souls is seen in His going after lost souls. We see this beautifully set forth by our Lord in Luke 15:4: *What man of you, having a hundred sheep, and having lost one of them, doth not leave the ninety and nine in the wilderness, and go after that which is lost, until he find it?* This is a part of the parable of the lost sheep.

There are three parables concerning the lost in the fifteenth chapter of Luke: the parable of the lost sheep, the parable of the lost coin, and the parable of the lost son. The parable of the lost sheep sets forth the love of Christ Jesus, the Good Shepherd, for the lost; the parable of the lost coin sets forth the love of the Holy Spirit for the lost; and the parable of the lost son sets forth the love of God the Father for the lost.

But we are concerned here only with the parable of the lost sheep and the love of Christ for the lost as it is pictured. This parable tells us that the incarnate Son of God *goes after the lost sheep until he finds it.* There is a wealth of meaning in these words, which we cannot stop to fully explain now. Jesus Christ *went after* lost souls. He not only watched for and welcomed opportunities when they came His way, but He also sought opportunities. He not only received the lost when they came to Him, but He also went after them. A true love for souls will always reveal itself in our going out in search of them. Are you going out and seeking the lost? Most of us think we are doing pretty well (and indeed we are doing better than the average professing Christian) when we deal with the lost when they come to church – when they come to us. But Jesus Christ went after them. Shouldn't we do the same?

A true love for souls will always reveal itself in our going out in search of them.

Some years ago in Chicago, a young woman who attended the Moody Church selected a block in a section of the city called

Little Hell with the resolution that she would call on every house and tenement, front and rear, in that block, and seek to lead all the lost ones she found to Christ. One day she rapped at a door, and a hoarse voice said, "Come in."

She entered. The room was very bare and lying on a wretched bed in an alcove off the room was a man dying of tuberculosis. She stepped to his side and said, "Are you a Christian?"

"No," he savagely replied, "I am an infidel." She said nothing more about Christianity but spoke a few kind words and left.

The next day she took him a pot of jelly; the next day a pot of jam; the next day some other delicacy. She kept this up for a month. Then one Sunday afternoon she came to me at the close of my Bible class and said, "Mr. Torrey, there is a man dying down on Townsend Street, and he is an infidel. I do not think he has long to live. I know you are busy and wish to go home to prepare for your evening service, but won't you come and say a few words to him before he dies?"

I hurried with her to this wretched tenement. She took me in, and after introducing me, she slipped away. I sat down by the dying man's bed and asked if I could read the Scriptures to him. He said I could. I read him some passages that tell of the love of God for the sinner. Then I read him passages that told how the Lord Jesus Christ had died on the cross of Calvary for our sins and how all our sins had been laid upon Him. I read John 3:16 where it tells not only of the love of God but also of how anybody wanting to be saved only has to believe in the Son of God. Then I asked him if I might pray with him. He said I could.

I knelt down beside that wretched bed and asked God to open that dying infidel's eyes to see that not only there was a God but that God also loved him. I asked God to help him see that because Jesus Christ, the Son of God, died for him, all he had to do to find forgiveness for his sins and be saved was to believe in the Christ who had died for him and had risen again. I asked God to lead this man to faith in Christ, and as I finished my prayer, he said, "Amen." Then as best as I could, I began to sing as I still knelt there:

> Just as I am! without one plea,
> > But that Thy blood was shed for me,
> And that Thou bidd'st me come to Thee,
> > O Lamb of God! I come! I come!

I sang on verse after verse, and when I reached the last verse the dying man joined in with me. Evidently, he had heard the hymn sometime in his childhood at church or Sunday school, and it still remained in his mind. Word for word he sang with me:

> Just as I am! Thou wilt receive,
> > Wilt welcome, pardon, cleanse, relieve,
> Because Thy promise I believe,
> > O Lamb of God! I come! I come![1]

I looked up and said, "Did you really come?"

He said, "I did." I arose and explained to him more fully from the Scripture the way of life and left him rejoicing in Christ. That very night he passed into eternity, a saved man, saved because a humble woman walked in the footsteps of her Master and *went out to seek and to save* the lost.

Finding His Joy and Satisfaction in Saving Lost Souls

We see the love of Jesus Christ for souls in that He found His joy and satisfaction in saving lost souls. We have a striking

---

1   Charlotte Elliott, "Just As I Am," 1835.

illustration of this in the chapter to which I have already referred, the fourth chapter of John.

You recall the early part of the story. As He talked with the woman who was an outcast, His disciples returned from the city, bringing food. They were surprised to find Him talking with a woman but said nothing until the woman left. Then they offered Him food and said unto Him, *Rabbi, eat,* to which He replied, *I have meat to eat that ye know not.*

The disciples turned to one another and said, *Hath any man brought him aught to eat?*

Then Jesus said unto them, *My meat is to do the will of him that sent me, and to accomplish his work* (John 5:31-34).

In other words, in this work of saving souls, He forgot weariness, hunger, and thirst. In it he found joy for His soul and even refreshment for His body. Is it so with you? Is saving souls your very food and drink?

On another occasion He was so taken up with the work that He had no time to *so much as eat bread. And when his friends heard it, they went out to lay hold on him: for they said, He is beside himself* (Mark 3:20-21). In this we see that Jesus so lost Himself in His work of saving souls that He neglected the ordinary needs of His body, until His friends thought He was insane.

We have another striking illustration of this in the ninth chapter of Luke. Jesus had heard of the death of John the Baptist, and His heart grieved over the loss of His cousin and friend. The apostles had just returned from a missionary tour and had *declared unto him what things they had done.* He took them aside into a secluded place for rest. But the multitudes saw Him going and followed Him, and His rest was given up. The striking thing comes out next where we read that *he welcomed them, and spake to them of the kingdom of God* (Luke 9:10-11).

What was rest to Him? Here was an opportunity to save

souls, and as much as He needed a time of rest, there was greater joy and satisfaction in saving the lost than in any recreation and rest He could find.

His Rejoicing in Finding Lost Souls

The love of Jesus Christ for souls is seen in His rejoicing with great joy over lost souls found. This is also seen in the parable of the lost sheep. In His own exact words we read: *When he hath found it* [the lost sheep], *he layeth it on his shoulders, rejoicing. And when he cometh home, he calleth together his friends and his neighbors, saying unto them, Rejoice with me, for I have found my sheep which was lost. I say unto you, that even so there shall be joy in heaven over one sinner that repenteth, more than over ninety and nine righteous persons, who need no repentance* (Luke 15:5-7).

> There was greater joy and satisfaction in saving the lost than in any recreation and rest Jesus could find.

A shepherd rejoices over his lost sheep when he finds it, and the woman rejoices over the coin lost from her marriage necklace when it is found again. The gold-hunter rejoices over the great nugget of gold that he takes out of the earth, and the merchantman seeking pearls rejoices over the one pearl of great price that he finds. But our Lord Jesus rejoices infinitely more over a lost soul found.

How cold and little interested most of us are when we deal with a soul; and if perchance we succeed in leading him to accept Christ, how listless and indifferent we are about it. If you should find a diamond worth $1,000, you would be so excited and so glad that you would hardly be able to sleep that night. But you find and win a soul for Christ, and it will awaken scarcely a ripple of enthusiasm. Not so with our Lord Jesus. When He found one lost sheep, *he layeth it on his shoulders, rejoicing. And when he cometh home, he calleth together his friends and his neighbors, saying unto them, Rejoice with me, for I have found my sheep which was lost.*

His Great Grief over Lost Souls

The love of Jesus Christ for souls is seen in the fact that He grieved with great grief over lost souls that refused to be saved. This is seen in many actions and many utterances of our Lord. For example, He said, *Ye will not come to me, that ye might have life* (John 5:40). To appreciate these words of our Lord, we need to remember the circumstances under which the words were spoken, and the tone, the look, and the gesture with which Jesus uttered them. The Lord Jesus came into this world to save men, to bring life to them. He went up and down His land, offering this life to men as a free gift. He was soon to die a death of agony and disgrace and most awful shame to make this life possible for them. He offered this life freely to all who would come to Him, but the great mass of men of that day, like the great mass of men today, would not come.

They would gather in enormous crowds to see His miracles, obtain healing for their bodies, and listen to His words. But they would not really come to Him. One day, surrounded by a great crowd of these miracle-seekers and curiosity-mongers, He stretched out His yearning arms toward them and cried, *Ye will not come to me, that ye might have life.*

How I wish I could reproduce the look, the tone, and the gesture with which He uttered those words – the look of tenderest compassion, the tone of sorrowing, heartbreaking love, and the gesture of infinite yearning. We have another illustration of the same thing in Matthew where He looked out upon Jerusalem and moaned, *O Jerusalem, Jerusalem, that killeth the prophets, and stoneth them that are sent unto her! how often would I have gathered thy children together, even as a hen gathereth her chickens under her wings, and ye would not!* (Matthew 23:37).

No woman ever grieved over her stolen jewels, and no mother ever grieved over a lost child as Jesus grieved over lost men who refused to be saved. No words can picture the agony that shot through the heart of Jesus Christ when men refused to come to Him that they might have life.

Are we like Him in this? Do we do everything in our power to bring men and women to a decision for Christ, and if they *will not come,* do our hearts break over them in yearning and pity and love, or are we peeved and indignant that they will not yield to our skillful persuasion? Oh, if only we had a love for souls like Jesus had, there would be many won. Some who have such a love are constantly winning souls.

The story has often been told, but it bears repeating, of the old deacon who had a great burden for an infidel blacksmith in his village. For months the deacon studied all the infidel arguments and the replies to them given in books of Christian proofs. Then he called on the blacksmith in his shop and engaged him in conversation, but the blacksmith was still more than a match for the deacon, and in a very few minutes he had the deacon silenced. Then the deacon broke into tears and said, "All I can say is, I have a deep spiritual concern for your soul."

The deacon went home and said to his wife, "Wife, I am a failure in God's work. I have been studying all the infidel arguments and answers to them for months and thought I had them all mastered. I went down to the blacksmith, but he whipped me to a standstill in only a few moments. I am a failure in God's work." Then he went to his room alone, just off the porch. Kneeling down, he said, "O God, I am a failure in your work. I have been studying for months to meet the arguments of the blacksmith, and I went to talk with him, but he squelched me.

Oh God, you know I have a love for the blacksmith's soul, but I am a failure in your work."

But no sooner had the deacon left the blacksmith's shop than the blacksmith stood in deep thought and went into his house. He said to his wife, "Wife, I thought I knew all the arguments for Christianity, but the deacon used an argument this morning I never heard before. He said he had a deep spiritual concern for my soul. What does he mean?"

The wife was a canny woman and replied, "You'd better go ask him."

The blacksmith hung up his apron and took a shortcut to the deacon's house. He came up on the porch just as the deacon was praying, and he heard the deacon's voice coming through the shutter: "O God, you know I am a failure in your work."

The blacksmith pushed the door open and said, "Deacon, you are no failure in God's work. You have used an argument I never heard before. You said you had a deep spiritual concern for my soul, and I have come to have you pray for me." If only all of us had a deep spiritual concern for the souls of lost men and women. If only we had a love like that of our Lord for the lost, so that we would grieve with great grief over lost souls that refused to be saved.

His Laying His Life Down to Save Souls

The love of Jesus Christ for souls is seen in the fact that He gladly laid down His life to save souls. This fact comes out repeatedly. For example, Jesus said, *I am the good shepherd: the good shepherd layeth down his life for the sheep* (John 10:11). It comes out again when He says, *The Son of man came not to be ministered unto, but to minister, and to give his life a ransom for many* (Matthew 20:28). Here is the crowning proof of our

Lord's consuming passion for the salvation of the lost – He laid down His life to save the lost, laid it down gladly.

There was but one way in which sinners could be saved and that was by an atonement made by One who could make a sufficient atonement. Without the sacrificed life of a fit person, *without shedding of blood,* there could be no remission of sins (Hebrews 9:22). The incarnate Son of God, the eternal God-become-man, was the only person of all the universe who, by reason of His twofold nature, human and divine, and His absolutely sinless character, could make that atonement. He said, "I will make it; I will pay the price of man's salvation. I will give up my life to be a substitute sacrifice for him. I will make propitiation by the shedding of my blood."

Here is the proof of our Lord's passion for the salvation of the lost – He laid down His life to save the lost.

Even here we should follow in His steps. *He that saith he abideth in him ought himself so to walk, even as he walked* (1 John 2:6). Not that we can make atonement. There is no need of that. An absolutely perfect and sufficient atonement has already been made. But it is often necessary for the saved to lay down their lives for the salvation of the lost. Are you ready to lay down your life for perishing men? Are you willing, if need be, to sacrifice your life so that the vile outcast or the lost thousands who are in the foul degradation of the blackest heathenism may be saved?

What we need today are men and women who are willing to follow Christ in His love for souls and to go out and lay down their lives so others may live eternally. Raising untold millions of dollars by the Interchurch World Movement, or any other movement, will avail nothing unless men and women come forward who really have the Spirit of Christ, the love for souls that Christ had, and because of their love for lost souls are willing to lay down their lives to save others.

Chapter 5

The Real Christ: His Compassion

*Let all the house of Israel therefore know assuredly,
that God hath made him both Lord and Christ,
this Jesus whom ye crucified.* (Acts 2:36)

*But a certain Samaritan, as he journeyed, came
where he was: and when he saw him, he was
moved with compassion, and came to him, and
bound up his wounds, pouring on them oil and
wine; and he set him on his own beast, and
brought him to an inn, and took care of him. And
on the morrow he took out two shillings, and gave
them to the host, and said, Take care of him; and
whatsoever thou spendest more, I, when I come
back again, will repay thee. . . . Go, and do thou
likewise.* (Luke 10:33-35, 37)

*He that saith he abideth in him ought himself also
so to walk, even as he walked.* (1 John 2:6)

So far we have studied four features of the picture that God
has drawn in His Word of the real Christ – His holiness,
His love for God the Father, His love for men, and His love

for souls. In this chapter we will study the fifth feature in that picture – His compassion. Though I have given considerable study to this subject in years past, I never dreamed until I went to work on the present chapter how much there was on the subject for the message.

This chapter is primarily for the benefit of the preacher. However, I hope it will mean as much for many of you as it has meant for me, as I have studied what God has to say on this subject in the picture He has drawn of the Christ in the four Gospels.

I wish to call your attention particularly to the second text, which we will study in more detail later. It is, as most of you doubtless recognize, taken from the parable of the good Samaritan. Anyone who understands that parable must see a picture of Jesus Christ Himself in it. He alone fully answers to the picture which He has drawn. He tells us what we should do, but in doing so, He states what He has already done.

What I have discovered regarding the compassion of the real Christ in the study of the picture God has given in the four Gospels we will arrange under two general categories: first, the objects of Christ's compassion, and second, the way in which the compassion of the Christ was manifested.

The Objects of Christ's Compassion

Who were the objects of Christ's compassion?

The Multitudes
In the first place, He has compassion on *the multitudes*. In no less than five separate passages in the Gospels is the fact mentioned that Jesus Christ had compassion on the multitudes. One passage is Matthew 9:36: *But when he saw the multitudes, he was moved with compassion for them, because they were distressed*

and scattered, as sheep not having a shepherd. In this case, it was the fact that the multitudes were distressed and scattered as sheep having no shepherd that moved our Lord to compassion. That is a true description of the multitudes, the crowds, and the throngs today even as it was of the multitudes in our Lord's day. Oh, how unshepherded the great masses of men are today, and how sorely distressed they are.

Suppose our Lord Jesus were here today. How would He feel toward the heedless, thoughtless, unsatisfied, unshepherded multitudes that crowd our streets and parks, our places of amusement, our seaside and mountain resorts? How does our Lord feel today as He looks upon the unshepherded and distressed millions in China and other lands?

The attitude of our Lord toward the multitudes, the ordinary herd of men, and the masses as distinguished from the classes was in striking contrast to the attitude of the other religious leaders of the day, the scribes and Pharisees. They regarded the multitudes as *accursed* by God. When Nicodemus lifted his voice in favor of Jesus, the Pharisees said, *Hath any of the rulers believed on him, or of the Pharisees? But this multitude that knoweth not the law are accursed* (John 7:48-49). The attitude of many of our religious leaders today toward the multitudes is more like that of the Pharisees than it is like that of the Christ. What does it matter to them what becomes of the mob, the crowd, the masses, or the common herd if we can only gather people of intelligence and position and wealth and influence in our churches? There is no question how we ought to feel if we are real Christians, if we are followers of the real Christ. But how do *you* feel toward the great heedless masses of men and women, *the multitudes*?

In Mark 8:2 it was the fact that *the multitude* was hungry

> The attitude of many of our religious leaders today is more like the Pharisees than it is of the Christ.

that moved Christ to compassion. He said, *I have compassion on the multitude, because they have now been with me three days, and have nothing to eat.* Not only the spiritual destitution of men but their physical need as well appealed to the compassion of Jesus Christ.

In Matthew 14:14, the fact of seeing the crowd as a crowd moved our Lord to compassion. We read: *And Jesus went forth, and saw a great multitude, and was moved with compassion toward them.* Whenever Jesus saw a crowd of men, He was moved with compassion. A crowd of men is a pitiful sight. It represents so much sorrow, so much need, so much pain, and so much sin. What is your feeling when you look out upon a crowd? Is it mere curiosity? Is it contempt? Is it indifference? Or is it compassion? Judging from the context of this last passage, the sick seem to have especially drawn out the compassion of the Lord Jesus.

The Grieving

Jesus Christ had compassion on those who had lost loved ones. We see a beautiful and touching instance of this in Luke: *Now when he drew near to the gate of the city, behold, there was carried out one that was dead, the only son of his mother, and she was a widow: and much people of the city was with her. And when the Lord saw her, he had compassion on her, and said unto her, Weep not* (Luke 7:12-13).

The woman was a perfect stranger to our Lord, but as He saw her deep and bitter sorrow over the loss of her only son, His whole heart was stirred with compassion for her. He is just the same today: *Jesus Christ is the same yesterday and to-day, yea and for ever* (Hebrews 13:8). Ah, how many a lonely sorrower thinks no one cares. But Jesus cares.

How unlike Christ Jesus are the Christian Scientists. They have no compassion on the bereaved one. No, not for a moment.

"There is no such thing as death," they say. "Those who you think are dead have only passed on. You must not weep, and I won't weep with you."

It is true that in this instance our Lord Jesus told the woman not to weep, but it was not because her only beloved son of whom she was separated had passed on, but because he would be immediately restored alive to her. And at the tomb of Lazarus, as He saw Mary and Martha weeping over the death of their brother, Lazarus, He wept too, though He knew their sorrow was but for a moment and was founded on a misunderstanding, and that in a few minutes, it would be changed into exceeding joy.

Nevertheless, their sorrow was real, and as it was theirs, it was His also. Oh, what an utter difference there is between the conduct of the unmotherly "Mother Eddy," the false Christ, and her satellites toward the sorrowing, and the conduct of our Lord Jesus, the real Christ. One of the most loathsome features of Christian Science is its conduct toward the sorrowing. It is cold, heartless, brute-like, selfish, and utterly lacking in sympathy and compassion.

The Afflicted People

Jesus Christ had compassion on all men who were afflicted by any form of misfortune, misery, wretchedness, or degradation. In Matthew 20:34 we are told He had compassion on two blind beggars at the gate of Jericho: *And Jesus, being moved with compassion, touched their eyes; and straightway they received their sight, and followed him.*

In Mark we are told He had compassion on a poor demonized boy: *And oft-times it hath cast him both into the fire and into the waters, to destroy him: but if thou canst do anything, have compassion on us, and help us. And when Jesus saw that a multitude came running together, he rebuked the unclean spirit, saying unto him, Thou dumb and deaf spirit, I command thee, come out of him, and enter no more into him* (Mark 9:22, 25).

In Mark 1:40-41 we are told He had compassion on a leper: *And there cometh to him a leper, beseeching him, and kneeling down to him, and saying unto him, if thou wilt, thou canst make me clean. And being moved with compassion, he stretched forth his hand, and touched him, and saith unto him, I will; be thou made clean.* The world, even the religious world of that day, met the leper with repulsion and disgust and scorn; Christ met him with compassion. The world drew away from him; Christ drew toward him.

Every form of misfortune and misery touched His heart. He entered into it as if it were His own. Here again we see the wide difference between the real Christ and the Christ of Christian Science. Is a man sick? That awakens no sympathy in a Christian Scientist. No, it awakens only reproach. "You have no right to be sick," says the Christian Scientist. "You are in error. Sickness is only illusion, mortal thought."

But Jesus, the real Christ, had compassion on the sick and healed the real sickness and gave real healing, charging nothing. But the Christian Scientist practitioner heals an imaginary sickness (a sickness that **Jesus made other** is only in your mind) with an imaginary **men's sorrows His** healing (a healing that is also only in your **own sorrows.** mind) for real money (money that is not only in your mind but is also in the practitioner's palm and is put into the practitioner's bulging bank account).

Jesus Christ did not go about His work from a cold sense of duty, but His whole heart drew Him out toward those He helped and saved. His deeds of mercy cost Him something more than the sacrifice of leisure and the expenditure of effort and power. They cost Him heartaches. He made other men's sorrows His own sorrows, other men's agony His own agony, other men's sin and shame His own sin and shame. He could not look upon misery, sickness, pain, death, or sin without heart pangs.

We read in John 11:33: *When Jesus therefore saw her weeping, and the Jews also weeping who came with her, he groaned in the spirit, and was troubled.* Herein lay one great secret of His power. The misery we make our own we can comfort. The deficiency we make our own we can fully satisfy. The sin we make our own we can save another from. And this is what we read about our Lord Jesus in Paul's epistle to the Corinthians: *Him who knew no sin he made to be sin on our behalf; that we might become the righteousness of God in him* (2 Corinthians 5:21).

Real power to help men is an expensive thing, but anyone can have it who is willing to pay the price. But the one who is not willing to give up lightness of heart and take instead the burden of the heart over the world's sin and sorrow and shame may as well give up the thought of being a helper and, even more, a savior of men. Men cannot be saved by burning words, no, only by bleeding hearts.

In Dundee, Scotland, lived a lady of wealth and position, but she was also a Christian. Her interest was not in society and fashion, but in the poor, the needy, the fallen, and the outcast. One time this Christian lady became interested in a very depraved and hardened woman who was brought to the Home for the Fallen. This woman was dying from the results of her sin, but every attempt to interest her in the sinner's Friend and Savior, our Lord Jesus, had failed. Her time was growing very short.

The woman of wealth and position, the true follower of the real Christ, went to see her. As she tried to speak to her about the Savior she woefully needed, the dying woman only grew angry, more angry and more hard and bitter. With a breaking heart, the Christlike woman leaned over the dying sinner. She could not hold back the tears, and they fell from her eyes upon the cheek of the dying woman. Instantly that hard heart broke, and the outcast listened, saw Jesus, believed in Him, and was saved. Afterwards she said, "It was the tear that did it."

Oh, how this sorrow-stricken, sin-ruined world of ours, staggering toward its doom, needs men and women with a heart of compassion like our Lord's to tell it the story of the dying love and the resurrection power of the Son of God.

How the Compassion of the Real Christ Was Manifested

What we have just said brings us naturally to the way in which the compassion of the real Christ was manifested.

Sharing Sorrows
The compassion of Jesus Christ was manifested in making the sorrows of others His own. We see this in John 11:33-36: *When Jesus therefore saw her weeping, and the Jews also weeping who came with her, he groaned in the spirit, and was troubled, and said, Where have ye laid him? They say unto him, Lord, come and see. Jesus wept. The Jews therefore said, Behold how he loved him!*

As we have already seen, the sorrow of these bereaved sisters was only for a moment, and it was founded on a misunderstanding. In a few minutes it would be exchanged for the exceeding joy of having their brother restored to them alive and well. But their sorrow was real, and because it was theirs, it was Christ's also.

Speaking for God, Paul commands us to *weep with them that weep* (Romans 12:15). Oh, how little some of us do this. I have spoken of the utter heartlessness of the Christian Scientists, which is a matter of principle with them. It is an essential part of their religion, a close following in the footsteps of their lord, Mary Baker Eddy, but there is altogether too much heartlessness in professing, evangelical Christians which is diametrically opposed to their religion, to the example of their Lord, and to the teaching of the entire Bible. We are too busy, too busy sometimes in religious activities to stop to enter into the sorrow of others and to *weep with them that weep*. But the real Christ, in spite of all the work that was crowded into the three and one-half years of His very busy public life, was not too busy to stop to *weep with them that weep*.

We read in Matthew 20:30-34 that when He was hurrying forward on the most urgent business of His life, as He *stedfastly set his face to go to Jerusalem* (Luke 9:51) to His atoning death, two blind beggars in their misery called to Him. The disciples rebuked them and told them not to bother Jesus with their petty sorrows when He was on such an important mission, but Scripture says that *Jesus stood still, and called them*. Oh, if only we were more like Him, never too busy to stop to sympathize with and help the suffering, no matter how insignificant they may be in the eyes of the world.

Meeting Needs

The compassion of Jesus Christ was manifested not only in feelings and words but also in action – in self-sacrificing, persistent, thorough-going service to the needs of the destitute. We see this vividly and graphically in the parable of the good Samaritan. As already noted, the Good Samaritan is a picture of the Lord Jesus Christ Himself.

Note that when he saw the poor, wounded, robbed, stripped, naked, half-dead man, *he had compassion on him*, but that was not all. His compassion was not of that shallow, unreal sort that evaporates in sentiment and tears and expressions of sympathy. *[He] went to him, and bound up his wounds, pouring in oil and wine, and set him on his own beast, and brought him to an inn, and took care of him. And on the morrow when he departed, he took out two pence, and gave them to the host, and said unto him,*

Take care of him; and whatsoever thou spendest more, when I come back again, I will repay thee (Luke 10:33-35).

His compassion showed itself in action, self-sacrificing action. He put the wounded man *on his own beast.* He walked so the injured might ride; he went without so the injured might have; he took the injured to an inn, stayed with him, paid his bill, and provided for his future needs. His action was persistent and thorough. It did not only last for the passing hour, but he also stayed by the man until he could care for himself. Such was the compassion of the Christ of God and such should be ours: *He that saith he abideth in him ought himself also so to walk, even as he walked* (1 John 2:6).

Such was the compassion of the Christ of God and such should be ours.

Patient Teaching and Healing

The compassion of Jesus Christ toward the unshepherded was manifested in His patience – teaching them, healing the sick, and feeding the hungry. We see the first part of this in Mark 6:34: *And he came forth and saw a great multitude, and he had compassion on them, because they were as sheep not having a shepherd: and he began to teach them many things.* At this time He was weary and sore at heart. He had just heard of the death of His cousin and faithful friend, John the Baptist, and had gone aside with the disciples for quiet and rest. But He saw the crowd, the great unshepherded mob of common people, the neglected multitude. His heart was moved with compassion. Forgetting His own weariness and sorrow in the crying need of these neglected thousands of the masses, He spent the whole day in teaching them the great truths of the kingdom, which He made so simple that the common people could understand Him, and they heard Him gladly. He taught them before He fed them, for the needs of their souls were far deeper and far greater than the needs of their bodies.

So it is today. The intellectual and spiritual needs of the masses are far greater than their physical needs, and a wise, Christlike compassion will minister to their spiritual and moral needs before it does to their physical needs. It is often said that Jesus fed the bodies of men before He sought to teach and save them, but the inspired record tells us differently. Our Lord was not so foolish as to try to reach the superficial need before attending to the deeper spiritual need beneath it. Here is where the social-service enthusiasts are making a colossal blunder at home and in the foreign field. We'd do well to follow in our Master's footsteps.

But Jesus did not stop with ministering to the spiritual needs beneath their physical needs. He also ministered to their bodies; He ministered to their hunger and to their sickness. He fed and healed them. This we see in Matthew's account of the same incident: *And Jesus went forth, and saw a great multitude, and was moved with compassion toward them, and he healed their sick* (Matthew 14:14). *Then Jesus called his disciples unto him, and said, I have compassion on the multitude, because they continue with me now three days, and have nothing to eat: and I will not send them away fasting, lest they faint in the way* (Matthew 15:32).

Christianity exalts the spirit of man, but it does not forget or neglect the body. It first teaches and heals the spirit and then feeds and heals the body. Social service is all right if we put it in its right place. Our Lord's compassion began with the spiritual needs of the multitude, but it did not end there. The salvation that the real Christ brings is salvation for *spirit and soul and body* (1 Thessalonians 5:23), but it puts the spirit first. The manifestation of Christ's compassion in teaching the unshepherded is a manifestation we can all imitate, even though we have no money to feed the hungry or the gift of healing to help the sick. If you can do no more, you can find some unshepherded child on the street, and the streets are full of them, and teach him.

Touching

The compassion of Jesus Christ was manifested when He put forth His hand and touched the leper. We see this in Mark: *And there cometh to him a leper, beseeching him, and kneeling down to him, and saying unto him, If thou wilt, thou canst make me clean. And being moved with compassion, he stretched forth his hand, and touched him* (Mark 1:40-41).

When one stops to reflect upon this incident and our Lord's action, there is something exquisitely beautiful in it. For years that leper had not felt the touch of a clean and loving hand. His nearest friends and dearest relatives shrank from him. He was indeed an outcast; whenever a clean man or woman approached him, he was forced to betray his misfortune and the danger of contact with him by crying out in a strained, hoarse voice, "Unclean, unclean." And now he approached Jesus and cried, *If thou wilt, thou canst make me clean.* And the heart of our Lord went out to him in infinite compassion, and He stretched forth His hand and touched him, and by that touch He healed him.

> You cannot save sinners at the end of a forty-foot pole.

Many today need and long for the touch of a clean hand, and that touch will heal them. Ah, but we shrink away. How the holy woman shrinks away from the vile woman on the street; how the holy man shrinks from the touch of the licentious man, the moral leper. And that is natural and that is right to a certain point. But, if you desire to help and save, then compassion must triumph over moral aversion, and we must get near the sinner and reach out our hand and *touch* him. You cannot save sinners at the end of a forty-foot pole. You must get within touching distance; you must touch.

When Mr. Alexander and I were in Bolton, England, we had a midnight sweep of the streets: we gathered the drunkards whom the taverns dumped into the street at that hour, formed a procession, and brought them to the armory. Three or four thousand men and women, many of them very drunk, were brought into the building. It was an awful-looking company of men and women. Mrs. Alexander had found a degraded, bloated, loathsome-looking woman on the street; she sat with her during the meeting and dealt with her in the discussion after the meeting. This repulsive-looking woman turned to Mrs. Alexander and said, "You do not love me."

Mrs. Alexander replied, "Yes, I do."

"Kiss me, then," she cried, and Mrs. Alexander kissed her and won her for Christ.

On one of my last visits to Chicago, a man came to me whom I had known years before. John Woolley had sent him to me the first time; he had sent him hundreds of miles to be helped, after he had professed conversion. He had been a drunkard and a crook, and he soon went back into his drunkenness and crookedness. Attempt after attempt was made by man after man to rescue him, but all attempts failed. He simply manipulated the people who tried to help him. Years had been spent in the attempt to rescue him, and I had not seen him for years until that night.

He came to me as I stepped down from the platform and said to me, "Mr. Torrey, I am a saved man now. I have been saved for some time, and I am helping to save others, but I am very ill with tuberculosis. I wanted to see you before I die, so I have come over tonight for that purpose. I have a good position. I need nothing, but what I wanted to tell you was this: I have never forgotten the day you knelt beside me and put your arm around me and talked to me and prayed for me. I have fallen repeatedly since that time, but how often I have felt your arm around me. Even in the prison cell, I have felt your arm around me, and, Mr. Torrey, that is what led me at last to accept Christ and be saved. Oh yes, in the prison cell, the memory of it helped me, and it saved me at last. I am dying; I don't have many months to live, but I felt I must tell you this before I died."

Friends, this world is full of men like that and full of women like the one Mrs. Alexander kissed. They are longing for real compassion, the compassion that gets right alongside them and touches them and saves them. The man of whom I spoke was one of the most unlikely men to be helped by such an act, of all the outcasts I have ever known. Never did I feel more like telling a man to be gone and never let me see him again than I did with that man. I knew he was a crook. I knew he was a professional worker of kindhearted people, and those like that are among the most hopeless of men; but compassion conquered and saved even him.

Welcoming and Forgiving

What we have said leads naturally to the fifth way in which the compassion of Jesus Christ was manifested. It was manifested in welcoming and pardoning the sinner and bidding the sinner to go in peace. This we see in an instance to which I referred earlier of the love of the real Christ for men. We find it in the seventh chapter of Luke. A woman who was a notorious outcast at Capernaum may have heard Jesus say, *Come unto me, all ye that labor and are heavy laden, and I will give you rest* (Matthew 11:28). If so, those words had gone straight to her heart and led her to believe in Him. When the crowd broke up, she followed Him down the street and saw Him enter the house of Simon the Pharisee. Then she hurried home and took her most cherished possession, her costly alabaster box of expensive ointment. She hurried back to Simon's house, stole in through the open door, approached Jesus as He reclined at the table, leaned over His bare feet, and wet them with her tears and wiped them with her hair.

Simon the Pharisee and the other guests were shocked that our Lord would even allow such a woman, so notorious a sinner, to touch Him. But the heart of our Lord Jesus went out in compassion toward the woman, vile and sunken though she had been, and looking into those tear-dimmed eyes, He said to her, *Thy sins are forgiven,* and then He said to her, *Thy faith hath saved thee; go in peace* (Luke 7:48, 50). So we too, instead of turning from the sinful in disgust, or repelling them when they repent and wish to do better, must welcome them and bid them to go in peace.

We will close this chapter with this manifestation of the compassion of our Lord, but just these two thoughts in closing. First, Jesus Christ, the real Christ, the only real Christ, is just the same today as when He walked this earth: *Jesus Christ is the same yesterday and to-day, yea and for ever* (Hebrews 13:8).

Second, *He that saith he abideth in him ought himself also so to walk, even as he walked* (1 John 2:6). It is difficult to follow our Lord Jesus, the Christ of God, in His holiness, but for many of us, it is far more difficult to follow Him in His compassion. This is not a compassionate age.

> It is difficult to follow our Lord Jesus in His holiness, but for many of us, it is far more difficult to follow Him in His compassion.

We may talk as we please about the "brotherhood of man"; we may multiply our humane societies and our Red Cross societies, but our almsgiving, our social service, and our general helpfulness is of an institutional character and lacks the warm, personal element. It lacks the touch of Christlike compassion.

We act through our various agencies instead of going forth as our Lord Jesus did by getting into actual living, loving, compassionate touch with the individual in sorrow, distress, bereavement, or sin in this sorrowing, brokenhearted world of ours. Even we preachers want men to be saved by preaching from the pulpit rather than by getting right in touch with you and your need and your sorrow and your sin – and church members follow in our steps. Oh friends, follow in the steps of the real Christ and mingle with men – the poor, the sorrowing, the sick, and the sinful. Make their sorrows your own, as Christ did. Then and then only, you can save them.

Chapter 6

The Real Christ: His Meekness

Let all the house of Israel therefore know assuredly,
that God hath made him both Lord and Christ,
this Jesus whom ye crucified. (Acts 2:36)

Take my yoke upon you, and learn of me; for I am
meek and lowly in heart: and ye shall find rest unto
your souls. For my yoke is easy, and my burden is
light. (Matthew 11:29-30)

Now I Paul myself entreat you by the meekness and
gentleness of Christ. (2 Corinthians 10:1)

Tell ye the daughter of Zion, behold, thy King
cometh unto thee, meek, and riding upon an ass,
and upon a colt the foal of an ass. (Matthew 21:5)

Thus far we have studied five features in the picture which God has drawn in His Word of the real Christ, the Christ of actual fact as distinguished from the Christ of man's fancies and dreams, the Christ of romance, the Christ that never did and never will exist and shouldn't exist. We have studied His holiness, His love for God the Father, His love for men, His love for souls, and His compassion. Now we will study the sixth feature in that picture, a feature that relates to His compassion, but which at the same time is quite distinct from it.

Our subject in this chapter is the meekness of Jesus Christ. Three of our four texts state and emphasize the fact that the Lord Jesus was meek. In the second text, His lowliness is put in close connection with His meekness, and at first I thought of combining these two in one chapter, but I found that the material was so abundant as to necessitate two chapters. Furthermore, though closely associated, they have entirely separate and distinct features. The meekness of Christ is one thing; His lowliness and humility are quite another thing.

What Is Meekness?

The first question that confronts us is, What is meekness? We shall find it is something quite different from the ordinary understanding of meekness. The thought that the word *meekness* conveys to the average mind, that indeed it formerly conveyed to my own mind, is that of "patient submissiveness under injustice and injury." Jesus displayed that quality, as we shall see when we come to study His humility, but that is not what the Bible means by *meekness*. The Greek word translated *meek* in our texts means "gentle" or "mild," according to its usage in Greek literature since the time of Homer. The word in its Bible usage means the same.

I have carefully researched the sixteen passages in the Bible in which the word and its derivatives are found. The contexts in which the word is found clearly show that the meaning of *meekness* is that attitude of mind that is opposed to harshness and contentiousness, the attitude of mind that shows itself in mildness and gentleness and tenderness in dealing with others.

The thought of gentleness in dealing with and correcting the errors of others is the predominant thought.

We see this in three of our texts. *Take my yoke upon you, and learn of me; for I am meek and lowly in heart: and ye shall find rest unto your souls* (Matthew 11:29). The thought here is that we will find rest in learning of Jesus because He is a gentle and not a harsh teacher and master.

This is more evident from the next verse: *For my yoke is easy, and my burden is light* (Matthew 11:30). The Greek word translated *easy* in this verse really means "mild," "kind," "pleasant," or "gracious."

That gentleness or mildness is the thought of the word in 2 Corinthians 10:1: *Now I Paul myself entreat you by the meekness and gentleness of Christ.* This is evident from the word with which it is coupled: *gentleness*. That gentleness, as distinguished from the warlike spirit, is the thought in Matthew 21:5: *Tell ye the daughter of Zion, behold, thy King cometh unto thee, meek, and riding upon an ass, and upon a colt the foal of an ass.* This is evident from His meekness being associated with His sitting on an ass, the beast of burden and service, as distinguished from the horse, which in the Bible is associated with war.

> **We will find rest in learning of Jesus because He is a gentle and not a harsh teacher.**

How the Meekness of the Christ Was Manifested

That the thought of gentleness, mildness, and tenderness in correcting the errors of others is the intention of God in speaking of the meekness of Christ will become more evident as we consider how that meekness was manifested.

Gentleness in Spiritual Dealings

The meekness of the Christ was manifested in His gentle dealing with those whose spiritual life was fragile and the flame of whose love for God was flickering. This is seen in Isaiah's prophetic vision of the coming Christ, which Matthew quotes and applies to Jesus of Nazareth in his Gospel: *A bruised reed shall he not break, and smoking flax shall he not quench* (Matthew 12:20; Isaiah 42:1-3). The feeble and flickering faith and love of many is compared here to the reed that is bruised and almost broken, and the wick that is smoking and almost extinguished. The Lord Jesus will treat such individuals not with the severity and sternness that will crush and extinguish them, but with the tenderness that will strengthen and cherish and fan them into flame.

This is a lesson we all need to learn in dealing with those who are young in the Christian life and weak in their faith. There is a great danger of discouraging these by expecting too much and demanding too much of them. Many who were once like a reed that was nearly broken are today a stalwart oak able to resist any violent storm, and many who were once like a smoldering wick about to go out are now brightly shining lights for God. But many well-meaning but tactless, self-sufficient, and unchristian zealots for the truth and for rightness crush the bruised reed and quench a smoking wick.

If only we were all more like our Lord in this. He used the most considerate, delicate, and exquisite tenderness in dealing with the broken; with gentle breath He encouraged the fire that was nearly gone out instead of blowing it out with a too-vigorous blast.

Gentle Forgiveness

In the second place, the meekness of the Christ was manifested in His gently telling the outrageous but penitent sinner that her sins were forgiven and to go in peace. We see this illustrated in the incident to which we referred in speaking of the compassion of Christ, the incident of the outcast woman of Capernaum recorded in Luke 7. When she came into the house of Simon where Jesus was reclining at the table, Simon and the other guests would have driven the woman from the house in righteous indignation because of her vile conduct in the past. But Jesus, looking into those tear-dimmed eyes, saw the dawning of a better life; He saw the sincere penitence and the budding faith in Himself and said to her, *Thy sins are forgiven,* and then again He said to the woman, *Thy faith hath saved thee; go in peace* (Luke 7:48, 50). Which are we more like, our Lord Jesus or Simon the Pharisee?

Many years ago, in my first pastorate at an outstation, a woman who had been a notorious sinner was converted and desired to be baptized by immersion. We gathered at a pool of water; I went down into the pool with the woman and buried her and her past beneath the baptismal waters, and she was raised again into newness of life. But some good people, really good people, I think, thought it was dreadful that I should baptize a woman like that, at least so soon. Though they were good people in many ways, in this they certainly were utterly unlike the Lord. Some of the saintliest people I have ever known were once the vilest of the vile, but fortunately for them, in the beginnings of their Christian life, they had fallen in with those who had learned something of the meekness of the Christ of God.

I know a man who is loved and honored by thousands, loved and honored as few are loved and honored in many states and on both sides of the Atlantic; but until he was forty-two years old, he was one of the wickedest and vilest of men. Then he was converted, very thoroughly converted, but extremely sensitive, weak, and easily discouraged. He came to Chicago while still a young convert and fell in with those who loved him and trusted him in spite of the black record of his past. But he still had grave discouragements.

One day he was sorely discouraged. He went to the house of a friend who had welcomed him to the fireside, yes, to the very heart of his own home circle. A little child who could scarcely talk ran eagerly to him, and he took her up in his arms. Throwing her arms around his neck, she whispered, "I love you, Coby." It was a message of hope and cheer from heaven, spoken from a child's lips. It was the catalyst that drove him to Christ; he went on to Christian service, a service in which he has been marvelously blessed. Suppose he had been received with severity, cold words, and suspicion, and excluded from that family circle. Where would he have been today?

Tenderness to the Fearful and Cowardly

The meekness of the real Christ was manifested in His tender words to a moral coward who had tried to steal a blessing from Him, unseen by any and confessing to none: *Daughter, thy faith hath made thee whole; go in peace, and be whole of thy plague* (Mark 5:33-34). This we see in the case of the woman who had the issue of blood. She had been ill for many years with a complaint that separated her from contact with the clean. She had heard of Jesus and *came in the crowd behind, and touched his garment. For she said, If I touch but his garments, I shall be made whole* (Mark 5:27-28).

She was a coward; she should have come openly; she should have confessed openly what He had done, before the confession was wrung from her. But the Lord Jesus did not disregard her on that account. He gently asked, *Who touched my garments?* To the disciples it seemed a foolish question, for many were crowding around Him and touching Him, but only one had really *touched* Him. The woman was full of fear and trembling. She knew she had done wrong. She was afraid He would drive her away and that she would lose the blessing. But with indescribable gentleness He turned to her and said, *Daughter, thy faith hath made thee whole; go in peace, and be whole of thy plague.*

Now, this woman was clearly in the wrong. She should have come openly and declared her need, and she should have confessed the healing. She richly deserved reproof. She deserved to go without the blessing that she sought to obtain in an underhanded way, without rendering to the Lord Jesus the acknowledgment and honor He so richly deserved; but how matchless was the gentleness and tenderness of our Lord! He did indeed bring out the public confession from her of her former need and present healing, but He did so gently.

Our Lord could be severe; He could be scathing in His rebukes, as we have already seen in studying His holiness, and as we will see again in studying His rugged manliness. But He could be more mild and gentle than the gentlest mother. That is an art we all need to learn more fully and to practice more constantly. You will say, "That is not my natural temperament." Then get a supernatural temperament; get it by supernatural grace that transforms a wrong temperament into a Christlike temperament; get it by the filling of the Holy Spirit. For *the fruit of the Spirit is love, joy, peace, longsuffering, kindness, goodness, faithfulness, meekness, self-control* (Galatians 5:22-23).

> Our Lord could be more mild and gentle than the gentlest mother. That is an art we all need to learn.

Gentleness in Rebuking Unbelief
The meekness of the Christ of God was manifested in the gentleness with which He rebuked the stubborn unbelief of a willful though honest doubter. We see this in the case of Thomas. You know the story as recorded in John. Recall how when our Lord appeared to the disciples on the evening of His resurrection,

Thomas was not with them. When he returned to them, all together the disciples cried, *We have seen the Lord.* Thomas said, *Except I shall see in his hands the print of the nails, and put my finger into the print of the nails, and put my hand into his side, I will not believe* (John 20:25).

A week passed and Thomas remained in his unbelief. But on the evening of the first day of the next week, the disciples were gathered together again, and this time Thomas was with them, and *Jesus cometh, the doors being shut, and stood in the midst, and said, Peace be unto you* to the whole company. Then He turned to Thomas and said to him so gently, *Reach hither thy finger, and see my hands; and reach hither thy hand, and put it into my side: and be not faithless, but believing* (John 20:26-27).

There are many doubters today, many stubborn, willful doubters, who can be won by treatment like that. But we try to pound our beliefs into their heads. We get angry, contentious, argumentative, and self-assertive when they will not accept our beliefs at once. We will never win them that way. We simply confirm them in their doubt and unbelief.

But you say, "They are unreasonable." Yes, they are unreasonable, and you are un-Christlike. Thomas was most unreasonable. He was stubborn; he was willful; he said, "Unless I am given the exact kind of proof I demand, I will not believe, no matter how sufficient other proofs are." But as unreasonable as Thomas was not to believe the competent testimony of the men whom he knew so well, and as willful as he was in trying to dictate what kind of proofs must be given, our Lord Jesus was gentle and kind. And soon we see Thomas on his knees looking up into the face of Jesus and crying, *My Lord and my God* (John 20:28).

I saw a man like that one summer in China. I watched him with keen and most astonished interest. He was gently courteous with everyone – with the Chinese as well as with the Europeans, with the Chinese coolie as well as with the Chinese gentleman, with the stubborn skeptic as well as with the enthusiastic believer in Christ – and he won everyone. I saw little children flock around him and drink in every word he spoke; I saw prominent scholars defer to him; I saw a proud Chinese gentleman yield to him and do with cheerfulness what he was very loath to do. Where had he learned this? He had learned it from the Lord Jesus to whom he had turned in such early boyhood that he didn't have the faintest recollection of when he was converted.

Many of us were converted later in life, and we had been harsh, overbearing, self-assertive, and domineering before we were converted. We have brought much of our severity and our domineering self-assertion and determination to influence everyone else to our point of view, whether they wanted it or not, into our new life. But we can learn better.

Tenderness in Rebuking Self-Confidence and Unfaithfulness
The meekness of the Christ was manifested in the tenderness with which He rebuked self-confidence, a consequent fall, unfaithfulness, and flagrant denial of Himself. The particular instance of this that we have in mind is, of course, that of Peter. You can read about it in John 21:15-17. Peter had said on the night before the crucifixion, *Though all men shall be offended because of thee, yet will I never be offended.* And he had said again, *Though I should die with thee, yet will I not deny thee* (Matthew 26:33-35). Remember how a little later, when faced with a charge made by a servant girl, *Art not thou also one of this man's disciples?* Peter's courage instantly vanished, and his protestations of loyalty were utterly forgotten (John 18:17). Remember how he denied his Lord three times, the last time with oaths and cursings.

Then, when Jesus was risen from the dead, Peter met Him

on the shores of Galilee. Breakfast was over, and our Lord asked Peter, *Simon, son of John, lovest thou me more than these?*

Peter answered, *Yea, Lord; thou knowest that I love thee.*

And Jesus said, *Feed my lambs.* Then again a second time Jesus asked, *Simon, son of John, lovest thou me?*

And again Peter replied, *Yea, Lord; thou knowest that I love thee.*

And Jesus said, *Tend my sheep.* Then a third time the Lord, looking into Peter's eyes, asked, *Simon, son of John, lovest thou me?*

And grieved, Peter answered, *Lord, thou knowest all things; thou knowest that I love thee.*

And Jesus said unto him, *Feed my sheep.*

How wonderfully tender it all was! Searching, it is true, but how tender! How gentle! And all the more effective because Peter was grieved, grieved all the more deeply because it was so gentle. Peter never forgot it; he never denied his Lord again. When standing before the very council that had condemned Christ to death, he said,

> *Ye rulers of the people, and elders, if we this day are examined concerning a good deed done to an impotent man, by what means this man is made whole; be it known unto you all, and to all the people of Israel, that in the name of Jesus Christ of Nazareth, whom ye crucified, whom God raised from the dead, even in him doth this man stand here before you whole. He is the stone which was set at nought of you the builders, which was made the head of the corner. And in none other is there salvation: for neither is there any other name under heaven, that is given among men, wherein we must be saved* (Acts 4:8-12).

How differently some of us would have treated Peter. We would have received him back, yes, but what a sound trouncing we would have given him first. I can imagine myself handling Peter and saying fiercely in "righteous indignation," "Simon, you coward, denying your Lord with oaths and curses. You ought to be ashamed of yourself. You ought to go and hide your head. You ought to hesitate to show yourself in the presence of His disciples." How unlike we are to Him whom we call our Lord.

Tender Reproof of His Betrayer

The meekness of the Christ was manifested in His tender and pleading reproof of His betrayer, Judas Iscariot. We see this in John: *[Jesus] was troubled in the spirit, and testified, and said, Verily, verily, I say unto you, that one of you shall betray me.* Later, after He had given the morsel to Judas, Satan entered into Judas. Jesus turned to him and said, *What thou doest, do quickly* (John 13:21, 27). What tenderness and what pleading there was in all this. We will feel it more if we try to imagine the tone in which Jesus said it.

> How differently some of us would have treated Peter. How unlike we are to Him whom we call our Lord.

It is true that in the case of Judas the meekness of our Lord failed to bring him to repentance, but the devil had already entered into Judas, and the devil is incorrigible, even before the meekness and gentleness of our Lord. We see the same thing once more in the garden when Judas came with the priests and soldiers to arrest Jesus and drag Him to trial and crucifixion. Judas brazenly approached Jesus and kissed Him in seeming affection, but in reality to mark Him as the one to arrest. Full of pity and a voice that was shaking with compassionate yearning, our Lord said, *Judas, betrayest thou the Son of man with a kiss?* (Luke 22:48). Our Lord would win Judas even yet if it were possible. If anything would have succeeded, that would have.

Praying for His Murderers

The meekness of the Christ was manifested in His praying for His murderers, the very ones whose hands nailed Him to the cross. The story is so well known to you that I hardly need repeat it. Jesus was hanging on the cross in awful agony, awful physical agony. But far more awful was the mental and spiritual agony; the whole weight of man's sins was laid upon *him who knew no sin* (2 Corinthians 5:21). He therefore recoiled in spiritual horror from sin as no other man ever recoiled, for no other was ever as holy as He.

The Father's face was being hidden from Jesus by the black cloud of your sins and mine. His heart was already breaking, and soon He would cry in an agony that no other man ever knew: *My God, my God, why hast thou forsaken me?* (Mathew 27:46). From the cross He looked down at those who had driven the nails into His hands and feet, hoisted the cross, and left Him hanging there. He saw them gambling for the garments they stripped from His poor body, and He uttered a prayer – not a prayer of condemnation but a prayer of wondrous pity: *Father, forgive them; for they know not what they do* (Luke 23:34).

The sublime simplicity and passion of the divine record impoverishes and makes impossible all attempts at human exposition. I do not need to attempt it. Meditate on it alone and never forget that *He that saith he abideth in him ought himself also so to walk, even as he walked* (1 John 2:6).

Chapter 7

The Real Christ: His Humility

*Let all the house of Israel therefore know assuredly,
that God hath made him both Lord and Christ,
this Jesus whom ye crucified.* (Acts 2:36)

*Take my yoke upon you, and learn of me; for I am
meek and lowly in heart: and ye shall find rest unto
your souls.* (Matthew 11:29)

*Now before the feast of the passover, Jesus know-
ing that his hour was come that he should depart
out of this world unto the Father, having loved his
own that were in the world, he loved them unto the
end. And during supper, the devil having already
put into the heart of Judas Iscariot, Simon's son,
to betray him, Jesus, knowing that the Father had
given all things into his hands, and that he came
forth from God, and goeth unto God, riseth from
supper, and layeth aside his garments; and he took
a towel, and girded himself. Then he poureth water
into the basin, and began to wash the disciples'
feet, and to wipe them with the towel wherewith
he was girded. Ye call me, Teacher, and, Lord: and
ye say well; for so I am. If I then, the Lord and the*

*Teacher, have washed your feet, ye also ought to
wash one another's feet. For I have given you an
example, that ye also should do as I have done to
you.* (John 13:1-5, 13-15)

*He that saith he abideth in him ought himself also
to walk even as he walked.* (1 John 2:6)

T hus far in our studies of the picture of the real Christ that
God has given us in His Word, we have looked at six features in the picture: His holiness, His love for God the Father,
His love for men, His love for souls, His compassion, and His
meekness. Now we will look at another feature intimately connected with His meekness.

Our subject is the humility of the real Christ, not the Christ
men dream about and paint from their own fancy upon canvas
or in words, but the Christ who actually existed, lived on this
earth among men, and left us an example that we should follow in His steps. The whole secret of a successful life here on
earth is walking in His steps. The more closely we follow in His
steps, the more successful our lives will be.

In the first of our texts, the fact is stated that Jesus of
Nazareth who was crucified by the rulers of His people was the
real Christ of God. In the second text, He states the fact that
He was *lowly of heart* or humble in heart. In the third text, we
have an amazing illustration of His humility and a statement
that those who desire to be His disciples must follow Him. And
in the fourth text, we have an emphatic teaching that anyone
who claims to abide in Him must make good his claim by
walking as He walked.

Humility is a distinctly Christian virtue. Humility was

regarded with contempt by the world's ethical philosophers until the Lord Jesus came and exemplified it in His own life and demanded it of all His followers. Xenophon, Plato, and Socrates all used the Greek word translated *lowly* in our text in contempt; they used it in the sense of cowardliness; Socrates used it frequently. And Epictetus, in some respects one of the greatest of Greek ethical philosophers, used a word derived from this as signifying "fainthearted," and so did the Jewish historian and moralist Josephus. To the Bible and to the Bible alone we owe the

> **His own glory was nothing to Jesus; the Father's glory was everything.**

exaltation of humility to a virtue, and we owe it preeminently to the teaching and example of Christ Jesus, the real Christ.

What Is Humility?

The first question that confronts us is, What is humility? This is a tremendously important question, for much that is dubbed humility is in reality cowardliness or hypocrisy, as in the classic example of Uriah Heep.[2] We shall see what real humility is by considering how the humility of the real Christ was manifested.

How Christ Manifested Humility

Sought Glory for the Father
The humility of the Christ of God was manifested in His not seeking His own glory. We see this in His own words in John, where He said, *And I seek not mine own glory* (John 8:50). His own glory was nothing to Jesus; the Father's glory was every-thing. It mattered nothing to Him that He might suffer in body or mind or reputation; if God was glorified by that suffering,

---

2   Uriah Heep is a character in Charles Dickens' *David Copperfield*. He is a hypocrite pretending to be humble, but his humility is a cover for cunning and deceitfulness.

He would choose it rather than the opposite. He compared His own glory to that of the Father: His glory was nothing, and God's glory was everything. *The Father is greater than I* was not merely a solitary utterance of Christ Jesus (John 14:28); it was also the keynote of all His thinking and living.

If we are to be at all like Him, we too must put our own glory behind our backs, completely out of sight. It must have absolutely no motive with us or modification of a motive. God's glory must not only be supreme but also all-encompassing. It must stand single and solitary as the only motive of our action in any part of our lives. There would be a reason for Jesus to claim His own glory, at least a secondary consideration after that of the Father; He possessed all the divine attributes in all their fullness, for in Him dwelt *all the fulness of the Godhead bodily* (Colossians 2:9). But even He, while equal with the Father in nature and attributes, never lost sight of His subordination to the Father, and He made His own glory absolutely nothing. Do we follow Him in this?

Avoided Praise
In the second place, the humility of the real Christ was manifested in His avoiding notoriety and praise. We see this first in a prophetic statement and afterward in the actual life of Christ Jesus here on earth. Isaiah put it in this way: *He will not cry, nor lift up his voice, nor cause it to be heard in the street* (Isaiah 42:2). Notoriety and praise were not something Jesus sought, they were something He shunned. He tried to perform even the miracles of healing, which His compassion compelled Him to do, under the cover of obscurity, repeatedly bidding the healed one to tell no one.

How unlike Him many of us are. He shunned notoriety, we court it. He sought to prevent the advertising of Himself; we have, or wish we had, an advertising bureau, and if someone gets more space than we do in the report of a "Victorious Life Conference," we are sorely offended. Ah, it is fine to dream and write songs about being Christlike. For some of us, it would not be so fine to really be so Christlike.

Associated with the Despised and Outcast

The humility of Jesus Christ was manifested in His associating in the most intimate way with the despised and outcast. We are told in Matthew that *it came to pass, as he sat at meat in the house, behold, many publicans and sinners came and sat down with Jesus and his disciples* (Matthew 9:10). There was nothing whatever of the social or religious snobbery about our Lord.

This was a cause of frequent complaint on the part of the religious aristocracy of the day, the Pharisees and scribes, that *this man* [Jesus] *receiveth sinners, and eateth with them* (Luke 15:2). Our Lord did not consider Himself either too good or too cultured or too blue-blooded (though He was of royal lineage even on the human side) to associate intimately in fellowship with the most despised classes. It was good red blood rather than blue blood, poisoned veinous blood, that coursed in His veins.

Today, even in the church, many consider themselves quite above intimate fellowship with some of their fellow church members. Some years ago, I attended a church service in an eastern city. On that morning, the church was receiving some poor missionary people as members. I had a friend in the congregation, a woman of wealth, culture, and social prominence, who was a member of the church. I noticed she did not rise when the members from the mission were welcomed into the fellowship of the church. I said to her afterwards, "Why didn't you stand when these members from the mission were received into the membership of the church?"

"Oh," she replied, "I could not say what the covenant says

regarding them. I have no intention of associating with them."
And yet she was a woman of a benevolent spirit far beyond the
average, a woman who was using her money largely for the
elevation of the poor.

It was not like this with our Lord; none were too poor or too
sinful for His companionship and fellowship. He knew He was
the Son and heir of the King of Kings and Lord of Lords, but
He had no sense of superiority toward the poorest and most
despised. In His association with the poorest and most sinful,
there was no nauseating, patronizing air of condescension that
so many display today when they have or think they have a
superior cultural or social position or morality or piety. Of all
snobs, the pious snob is the most offensive.

Submitted to Injustice
The humility of Jesus Christ was manifested in willing and joyous submission to outrageous injury and injustice. We have a
prophetic anticipation and prediction of this in Isaiah 50:5-6:
*The Lord Jehovah hath opened mine ear, and I was not rebellious,
neither turned away backward. I gave my back to the smiters,
and my cheeks to them that plucked off the hair; I hid not my
face from shame and spitting.* The prophecy of the humility of
the Christ who was to be, was fulfilled seven hundred years
later in the Christ who actually was, the Christ who lived here
on earth, Christ Jesus. He literally gave His back to those who
struck Him, and His cheeks to those who plucked off the hair,
and He did not hide His face from shame and spitting.

He submitted willingly, even joyfully, to outrageous injury
and injustice from men so that He might glorify God by saving the very ones who mistreated Him. How nearly like Him
are we in this? How nearly like Him do we care to be in this?

Remained Silent under Injury

Going a step further, the humility of Jesus Christ was manifested in silence under outrageous injury and injustice. We see this in another preview that Isaiah was given of the Coming One, the Coming Christ of God: *He was oppressed, yet when he was afflicted he opened not his mouth; as a lamb that is led to the slaughter, and as a sheep that before its shearers is dumb, so he opened not his mouth* (Isaiah 53:7). It is easy to bear grave injustice and outrageous injury if we can talk back and voice our injured innocence, our exalted sense of martyrdom. But to suffer and say nothing, not even call attention to what a pure and noble martyr you are, that is humility, the genuine article, the humility of the real Christ, Christ Jesus.

Stayed Silent under False Accusations

The humility of Jesus Christ manifested itself in absolute silence under false accusations. We are told this many times in the Word of God. Passages fill the memory of anyone who is familiar with the Bible. For example, Peter said, *Who, when he was reviled, reviled not again; when he suffered, threatened not; but committed himself to him that judgeth righteously* (1 Peter 2:23). And in Matthew we read: *Now the chief priests and the whole council sought false witness against Jesus, that they might put him to death; and they found it not, though many false witnesses came. But afterward came two, and said, This man said, I am able to destroy the temple of God, and to build it in three days. And the high priest stood up, and said unto him, Answerest thou nothing? what is it which these witness against thee? But Jesus held his peace* (Matthew 26:59-63).

Luke tells us: *Now when Herod saw Jesus, he was exceeding glad: for he was of a long time desirous to see him, because he*

> To suffer and say nothing, that is humility.

had heard concerning him; and he hoped to see some miracle done by him. And he questioned him in many words; but he answered him nothing. And the chief priests and the scribes stood, vehemently accusing him (Luke 23:8-10).

Our Lord Jesus did not defend His own good name; He left that to God. He *committed himself to him that judgeth righteously.* This is a lesson that we sorely need to learn. Many have learned it in part, but how often we forget it. So I emphasize again, *lest we forget.*

Ministered to All

The humility of Jesus Christ was manifested in His coming to minister and not to be ministered unto. One of the most significant and suggestive utterances that ever fell from His lips is that found in Matthew 20:28: *The Son of man came not to be ministered unto, but to minister, and to give his life a ransom for many.* That is humility – to really consider yourself the servant of all and to seek to serve all and be served by none. That is not natural, I suppose, to any of us. We wish to be waited upon rather than to wait upon others. And if we must serve, we are always looking forward to the time when we shall be served, and are constantly building castles in the air in which there are hosts of servants and we ourselves are the noblemen who are being served. Even in the church we covet the office where others dance in attendance upon us, instead of the lowly place of service in which we must do the bidding of others. The word *minister* originally meant "servant," but today it often means the "boss of the whole show," and we are greatly concerned about the prerogatives and dignity of, and the respect due, to the minister. And the word *deacon* also originally meant "servant," but now it means various degrees of dignity. Let us remember that the Master said, *The Son of man came not to be ministered unto, but to minister, and to give his life a ransom for many.*

Performed Humble Services

The humility of Jesus Christ was manifested in His performing the most humble and menial and repulsive services for others. He not only came to serve, though He actually did serve, but He also served in the lowliest forms of service. We see this in one of our texts:

> *Now before the feast of the passover, Jesus knowing that his hour was come that he should depart out of this world unto the Father, having loved his own that were in the world, he loved them unto the end. And during supper, the devil having already put into the heart of Judas Iscariot, Simon's son, to betray him, Jesus, knowing that the Father had given all things into his hands, and that he came forth from God, and goeth unto God, riseth from supper, and layeth aside his garments; and he took a towel, and girded himself. Then he poureth water into the basin, and began to wash the disciples' feet, and to wipe them with the towel wherewith he was girded* (John 13:1-5).

It was a slave's work that Jesus performed here. He and His disciples had come in from the dusty road and, in the Eastern custom, laid aside their sandals; but there was no servant to perform the customary and necessary foot washing for them. Not one of the disciples would do it for the others. Each felt it was beneath his dignity.

So our Lord in full consciousness of His divine authority and origin, *knowing that the Father had given all things into his hands, and that he came forth from God, and goeth unto God,* became like the humblest of servants. He arose, laid aside His garments, girded Himself with a towel, took the basin, and went from disciple to disciple washing their dirty feet.

I wonder why the painters who have given us their various representations of so many scenes in the life of Christ never painted that scene. In this context, our Lord specifically emphasized the fact that He had given us an example that we should do as He had done. How closely are you imitating the example that Jesus left? Would you rather be a minister by preaching sermons to a crowd of gaping admirers, or a minister by washing the sore and foul feet of some afflicted child of God? "Oh," but you say, "my social position and official dignity will not permit me to stoop to service of that character."

> Our Lord specifically emphasized the fact that He had given us an example that we should do as He had done.

Remember what we are told about Jesus in this regard, that it was with the full knowledge of His divine authority that *the Father had given all things into his hands,* and the full knowledge of His divine origin, mission, and destiny *that he came forth from God, and goeth unto God* that He did all this.

I once knew a young woman in Christian work in Chicago. For some reason I did not have a very high estimate of the depth of her devoutness. She belonged to a well-known family, and I imagined that she was altogether too conscious of it. But one day someone came and told me how she had gone into one of the poorest parts of Chicago called Little Hell. She found a poor, afflicted person in bed with sore and vile feet; she had unbound those feet with her own hands and cheerfully and pleasantly and thoroughly washed them. From that day on, I could not have had a higher estimation of the real Christlikeness of that young woman.

Chose the Lowest Level

As the ninth example, the humility of the Christ of God was manifested in His choosing the lowliest place of contempt as a slave instead of the loftiest place of glory as God. This choice of our Lord predated His entry into human history as an integral part of it all. It began in the eternal glory. We read it in that marvelous statement of Paul, which we have had occasion to quote so often: *Who, existing in the form of God, counted not the being on an equality with God a thing to be grasped, but emptied himself, taking the form of a servant, being made in the likeness of men* (Philippians 2:6-7). Oh, what sublime humility that was, stooping from the glory of occupying the throne of the universe, the center and object of angelic, cherubic, and seraphic worship, to take the form of a servant.

It is in this context that Paul exclaims with tremendous emphasis: *Have this mind in you, which was also in Christ Jesus* (Philippians 2:5). Yes, this is the mind of the real Christ, the mind of the Master, not primarily some doctrinal statement of faith, no matter how rigidly and completely orthodox. This is speaking of the mind of surrendering the very highest position and taking the very lowest, forsaking the place of highest honor and seeking the place of lowest and most effective service.

In the verses that follow, we see that He revealed His true humility by seeking the lowest place any man ever occupied, and that our Father *highly exalted him, and gave unto him the name which is above every name; that in the name of Jesus every knee should bow, of things in heaven and things on earth and things under the earth, and that every tongue should confess that Jesus Christ is Lord, to the glory of God the Father* (Philippians 2:9-11).

Obeyed unto Death

And last, the humility of Jesus Christ was manifested in His being *obedient unto death, even the death of the cross*

(Philippians 2:8 KJV). This is the climax of the previous thought. Let me repeat it: *And being found in fashion as a man, he humbled himself, becoming obedient even unto death, yea, the death of the cross* (Philippians 2:8 ASV). Here we reach the highest point of Christ's lowest humility, not merely God becoming man, the highest of all lords becoming the lowest of all servants, but also the holiest of all becoming the Sin-Bearer of the vilest of sinners. No other one who ever occupied by natural, divine, and eternal right so high a position of dignity, honor, glory, and worship as He did ever stooped to so low a depth of agony and shame, accursed of God and man. I repeat, it is in this context that the Spirit of God through Paul said, *Have this mind in you, which was also in Christ Jesus* (Philippians 2:5). And John also had this in mind when he said, *He that saith he abideth in him ought himself also to walk even as he walked* (1 John 2:6).

Chapter 8

The Real Christ: His Manliness

Let all the house of Israel therefore know assuredly, that God hath made him both Lord and Christ, this Jesus whom ye crucified. (Acts 2:36)

And it came to pass, when the days were well-nigh come that he should be received up, he stedfastly set his face to go to Jerusalem. (Luke 9:51)

Judas then, having received the band of soldiers, and officers from the chief priests and the Pharisees, cometh thither with lanterns and torches and weapons. Jesus therefore, knowing all the things that were coming upon him, went forth, and saith unto them, Whom seek ye? They answered him, Jesus of Nazareth. Jesus saith unto them, I am he. . . . Jesus answered, I told you that I am he; if therefore ye seek me, let these go their way. (John 18:3-5, 8)

Now is my soul troubled; and what shall I say? Father, save me from this hour. But for this cause came I unto this hour. Father, glorify thy name. (John 12:27-28)

*He that saith he abideth in him ought himself also
so to walk, even as he walked.* (1 John 2:6)

We have already studied seven features of the picture God has drawn in His Word of the real Christ: His holiness, His love for God the Father, His love for men, His love for souls, His compassion, His meekness, and His humility. The last three – His compassion, meekness, and humility – are very closely associated. But now we will study a marked characteristic of our Lord that is of a different sort – His manliness.

In most of the paintings of our Lord, the face is not only to a marked degree womanly, but it is also positively effeminate and weak. The same is true of the pictures of Christ Jesus drawn in words in many pulpits. That is not a true picture of the real Christ. I cannot endure the paintings of the face of Christ; they make me indignant. They dishonor my Lord. Gentle He was as we have already seen, and gentleness is more frequently a characteristic of women than of men, of mothers, wives, and daughters rather than of fathers, husbands, and sons. But while He was more gentle than the gentlest mother,

While Christ was more gentle than the gentlest mother, He was at the same time the strongest and most vigorous of all the sons of men.

the gentlest person who ever lived on this earth, the one true and perfect gentleman, He was at the same time the strongest and most vigorous of all the sons of men. Gentleness, humility, and meekness are seldom found coupled with energy and vigor.

I do not think that the term *manliness* accurately describes what I mean, for many women display many of the qualities I am about to describe more fully than most men. What we men, in our presumption and arrogance and self-sufficiency, call manliness is just as much, if not more, womanliness. But I use the term *manliness* because it comes closer to describing what I mean than any other term of which I can think.

I recall reading a book more than forty years ago called *The Manliness of Jesus*. I have entirely forgotten the contents of that book. Nevertheless, the book made a deep impression upon me at the time, and I presume it suggested the title of this chapter. Just what I mean by *manliness* will be clear as we consider how the manliness of the real Christ, not the Christ that artists paint from their own fancy but the Christ who actually lived on this earth and whose perfect portrait God has drawn in the Bible, was manifested.

His Absolute Fearlessness

In three of our five texts, we see that the manliness of Christ was manifested in His absolute fearlessness in the face of gravest peril. We often see this in the story of His life on earth. For example, consider the second text: *And it came to pass, when the days were well-nigh come that he should be received up, he stedfastly set his face to go to Jerusalem* (Luke 9:51). Our Lord knew He was going to Jerusalem to face shame, suffering, agony, and death. No other person ever walked this earth who naturally shrank from death as He did, for no other who walked this earth was as full of life as He was. But He looked the fast-approaching suffering, agony, shame, and death right in the eye without flinching and marched to meet it, to feel its sting, and to conquer it.

We see the same thing from a different angle in John:

> *Judas then, having received the band of soldiers,*
> *and officers from the chief priests and the Pharisees,*
> *cometh thither with lanterns and torches and*

weapons. Jesus therefore, knowing all the things that were coming upon him, went forth, and saith unto them, Whom seek ye? They answered him, Jesus of Nazareth. Jesus saith unto them, I am he. And Judas also, who betrayed him, was standing with them. When therefore he said unto them, I am he, they went backward, and fell to the ground. Again therefore he asked them, Whom seek ye? And they said, Jesus of Nazareth. Jesus answered, I told you that I am he; if therefore ye seek me, let these go their way (John 18:3-8).

The underlying significance of these words spoken under such circumstances is so evident that they need no comment.

Again we see much the same thing in John 12:27-28: *Now is my soul troubled; and what shall I say? Father, save me from this hour. But for this cause came I unto this hour. Father, glorify thy name.* The shadow of the cross lay across the pathway Jesus trod from the beginning of His public ministry. This is evident from His words in John 2:19: *Destroy this temple, and in three days I will raise it up,* which He uttered on His first visit to Jerusalem after the beginning of His public ministry. But He discerned from the outset the cross with all its unutterable horrors, horrors inconceivable to our finite minds. He marched toward it without swerving for one moment even an inch from the path God had marked out, undeceived or misled by the popularity that His benevolent ministry had begun.

> **Jesus discerned from the outset the cross with all its unutterable horrors.**

In this manly fearlessness, we must follow Him. In the face of the gravest peril, we must follow Him, for He has said in Matthew 16:24: *If any man would come after me, let him deny himself, and take up his cross, and follow me.*

The Boldness of His Utterances

The manliness of the Christ of God was manifested in the bold-ness of His utterances. We see this in His demeanor and in His words before the high priest Annas, and the Roman governor Pilate, as John has pictured them:

The high priest therefore asked Jesus of his disciples, and of his teaching. Jesus answered him, I have spo-ken openly to the world; I ever taught in synagogues, and in the temple, where all the Jews come together; and in secret spake I nothing. Why askest thou me? ask them that have heard me, what I spake unto them: behold, these know the things which I said. And when he had said this, one of the officers stand-ing by struck Jesus with his hand, saying, Answerest thou the high priest so? Jesus answered him, If I have spoken evil, bear witness of the evil: but if well, why smitest thou me? Pilate therefore entered again into the Praetorium, and called Jesus, and said unto him, Art thou the King of the Jews? Jesus answered, Sayest thou this of thyself, or did others tell it thee concerning me? Pilate answered, Am I a Jew? Thine own nation and the chief priests delivered thee unto me: what hast thou done? Jesus answered, My king-dom is not of this world: if my kingdom were of this world, then would my servants fight, that I should not be delivered to the Jews: but now is my kingdom not from hence. Pilate therefore said unto him, Art thou a king then? Jesus answered, Thou sayest that I am a king. To this end have I been born, and to this end am I come into the world, that I should bear witness unto the truth. Every one that is of the truth heareth my voice (John 18:19-23, 33-37).

When Pilate therefore heard this saying, he was the more afraid; and he entered into the Praetorium again, and saith unto Jesus, Whence art thou? But Jesus gave him no answer. Pilate therefore saith unto him, Speakest thou not unto me? knowest thou not that I have power to release thee, and have power to crucify thee? Jesus answered him, Thou wouldest have no power against me, except it were given thee from above: therefore he that delivered me unto thee hath greater sin (John 19:8-11).

Even more startlingly bold are His words before Caiaphas:

And they that had taken Jesus led him away to the house of Caiaphas the high priest, where the scribes and the elders were gathered together. Now the chief priests and the whole council sought false witness against Jesus, that they might put him to death; and they found it not, though many false witnesses came. But afterward came two, and said, This man said, I am able to destroy the temple of God, and to build it in three days. And the high priest stood up, and said unto him, Answerest thou nothing? what is it which these witness against thee? But Jesus held his peace. And the high priest said unto him, I adjure thee by the living God, that thou tell us whether thou art the Christ, the Son of God. Jesus saith unto him, Thou hast said: nevertheless I say unto you, Henceforth ye shall see the Son of man sitting at the right hand of Power, and coming on the clouds of heaven (Matthew 26:57, 59-64).

His Warrior Spirit

The manliness of the Lord Jesus was manifested in His warrior spirit. The Lord Jesus came *to heal the brokenhearted* (Luke 4:18), to comfort the sorrowing and heavy-laden (Matthew 11:28), and to gently bind up all the gaping wounds of humanity. But He also came to be the dauntless leader in the fiercest fight the universe has ever known. We see this repeatedly. Matthew 10:34 will probably serve to illustrate this as well as any passage in God's record: *Think not that I came to send peace on the earth: I came not to send peace, but a sword.* Jesus Christ was indeed the Prince of Peace, but He was also the Prince of warriors. The hymn "The Son of God Goes Forth to War" has a great truth in it, but this hymn is also just as true:

> Majestic sweetness sits enthroned
> Upon the Savior's brow;
> His head with radiant glories crowned,
> His lips with grace o'erflow.[3]

The peace the real Christ preached was peace through victorious warfare. To be a true follower of Jesus, the Christ of God, one must be a fearless fighter as well as a gentle comforter. And today the fight is hotter than ever before in this old world's history, for the end draws near, and Satan rages, for he knows his time is short. Today we need, we sorely need, warrior Christians. If we are to preach a full gospel, we must preach a gospel of hard, fierce, but completely victorious warfare.

To be a true follower of Jesus, one must be a fearless fighter as well as a gentle comforter.

---

3   Samuel Stennett, "Majestic Sweetness Sits Enthroned," 1787.

His Fearless Frankness

The manliness of Christ Jesus was manifested in His utter and fearless frankness in dealing with men. We see this illustrated many times. For example: *And as they went on the way, a certain man said unto him, I will follow thee whithersoever thou goest. And Jesus said unto him, The foxes have holes, and the birds of the heaven have nests; but the Son of man hath not where to lay his head* (Luke 9:57-58).

We see it again later in Luke:

> *Now there went with him great multitudes: and he turned, and said unto them, If any man cometh unto me, and hateth not his own father, and mother, and wife, and children, and brethren, and sisters, yea, and his own life also, he cannot be my disciple. Whosoever doth not bear his own cross, and come after me, cannot be my disciple. For which of you, desiring to build a tower, doth not first sit down and count the cost, whether he have wherewith to complete it? Lest haply, when he hath laid a foundation, and is not able to finish, all that behold begin to mock him, saying, This man began to build, and was not able to finish. Or what king, as he goeth to encounter another king in war, will not sit down first and take counsel whether he is able with ten thousand to meet him that cometh against him with twenty thousand? Or else, while the other is yet a great way off, he sendeth an ambassage, and asketh conditions of peace. So therefore whosoever he be of you that renounceth not all that he hath, he cannot be my disciple* (Luke 14:25-33).

Our Lord concealed nothing. He wanted all to know the very worst as well as the very best. While He longed for disciples because He knew that discipleship of Him meant infinite and eternal blessing for them, He would not have one person become His disciple without a full understanding of the tremendous cost of discipleship. He wanted them to have a clear and full comprehension of all the shame, suffering, and loss that would be involved in following Him.

This is a lesson that modern evangelists and preachers need to learn. We are constantly making improvements on what one gains by coming to and accepting Christ. Our Lord Jesus declared what one loses by coming to Him. He appealed to the heroism and self-sacrifice of men as well as their longing for peace, joy, and infinite reward.

> There is great need today that we preach a gospel of self-sacrifice and not a gospel that seeks to minimize the sacrifices.

There is great need today that we preach a heroic gospel of self-sacrifice and not a gospel that seeks to minimize the sacrifices involved in coming to Christ, or to transform the church that Christ Jesus founded, the crucified Christ, into a competitor with the dance hall, the card club, vaudeville, and the movie theaters.

His Uncompromising Attitude toward Sin

The manliness of Jesus Christ was manifested in His uncompromising attitude toward sin in all its forms. This is seen in that terse but meaningful utterance of His recorded in John 8:34: *Jesus answered them, Verily, verily, I say unto you, Every one that committeth sin is the bondservant of sin.* Sin was always sin in the eyes of Jesus. There was no such thing as excusable sin or venial sin or little sin in His estimation. Sin was always – whatever the particular sin might be – the same hateful, abominable, ruinous, enslaving thing. *Every one that committeth sin* [whatever the sin may be] *is the bondservant of sin*. He had compassion upon sinners of all sorts. He hated and denounced sin in all its forms. There was none of that namby-pamby, milk-and-water, half-admiring, half-diminishing atti-tude toward some forms of sin that is so common even among certain classes of professing Christians today.

He never called a carnival of lust a "romance," as our news-papers do almost every day. No, listen to His blistering words: *Every one that putteth away his wife, and marrieth another, committeth adultery: and he that marrieth one that is put away from a husband committeth adultery* (Luke 16:18). Sin was sin – hideous, loathsome, enslaving. He cries, *I tell you, . . . except ye repent, ye shall all likewise perish* (Luke 13:3-5). He pardoned sin when it was repented of, but He sternly added, *Sin no more, lest a worse thing befall thee* (John 5:14; 8:11).

His attitude toward sin was unyielding, strong, virile, uncompromising, and never condoning. This is a lesson that we need to learn. Sometimes because of our fondness for the sinner, because he is dear to us by ties of relationship, or from our very desire to be like our Lord in His compassionate deal-ings with sinners, we are tempted to condone the sins of some, even gross sins. That is utterly un-Christlike. He never did.

His Unbending Firmness

The manliness of Christ Jesus is seen in His unbending firm-ness. For example: *And he said unto another, Follow me. But he said, Lord, suffer me first to go and bury my father. But he said unto him, Leave the dead to bury their own dead; but go thou and publish abroad the kingdom of God. And another also said, I will follow thee, Lord; but first suffer me to bid farewell to them that are at my house. But Jesus said unto him, No man, having put his hand to the plow, and looking back, is fit for the kingdom of God* (Luke 9:59-62).

The requests of these two men seem reasonable at first, but not to Jesus. He had made a demand upon these men for immediate action. The call was not only important but also imperative, and the Lord Jesus did not yield one inch.

Leave the dead to bury their own dead, He gently but firmly said. And then: *No man, having put his hand to the plow, and looking back, is fit for the kingdom of God.* What manly positiveness and firmness we see in this. There was nothing of the weak, vacillating, babbling, sentimental, ethical culturist and moral liberalist about Him. He was a man, a full-grown man, every inch a man, God's pattern man.

The Severity of His Rebukes

The manliness of Christ Jesus was manifested in the severity with which He denounced hypocrisy, pretense, self-righteousness, self-sufficiency, self-deception, and unadmitted sin. We see this in frequent occurrences described in the brief record of His life on earth. For example: *And the Pharisees, who were lovers of money, heard all these things; and they scoffed at him. And he said unto them, Ye are they that justify yourselves in the sight of men; but God knoweth your hearts: for that which is exalted among men is an abomination in the sight of God* (Luke 16:14-15).

How severe and searching these words of our Lord were, especially when we remember to whom they were spoken; He spoke to the men who prided themselves not only upon the thoroughness and rigidity of their orthodoxy, but also upon the strictness of their morality and the loftiness of their ideals of holy living.

But look at something even more severe and stern:

But woe unto you, scribes and Pharisees, hypocrites! because ye shut the kingdom of heaven against men: for ye enter not in yourselves, neither suffer ye them that are entering in to enter. Woe unto you, scribes and Pharisees, hypocrites! for ye devour widows' houses, even while for a pretence ye make long prayers: therefore ye shall receive great condemnation. Woe unto you, scribes and Pharisees, hypocrites! for ye compass sea and land to make one proselyte; and when he is become so, ye make him twofold more a son of hell than yourselves. Woe unto you, ye blind guides, that say, Whosoever shall swear by the temple, it is nothing; but whosoever shall swear by the gold of the temple, he is a debtor. Ye fools and blind: for which is greater, the gold, or the temple that hath sanctified the gold? (Matthew 23:13-17).

And still further down in the chapter we read:

Woe unto you, scribes and Pharisees, hypocrites! for ye tithe mint and anise and cummin, and have left undone the weightier matters of the law, justice, and mercy, and faith: but these ye ought to have done, and not to have left the other undone. Ye blind guides, that strain out the gnat, and swallow the camel! Woe unto you, scribes and Pharisees, hypocrites! for ye cleanse the outside of the cup and of the platter, but within they are full from extortion and excess. Thou blind Pharisee, cleanse first the inside of the cup and of the platter, that the outside thereof may become clean also. Woe unto you, scribes and Pharisees, hypocrites! for ye are like

unto whited sepulchres, which outwardly appear
beautiful, but inwardly are full of dead men's bones,
and of all uncleanness. Even so ye also outwardly
appear righteous unto men, but inwardly ye are full
of hypocrisy and iniquity. Ye serpents, ye offspring
of vipers, how shall ye escape the judgment of hell?
(Matthew 23:23-28, 33).

Is this the same Christ Jesus that we saw when we studied His compassion or when we studied His meekness? Yes, this is the very same Jesus, Jesus the real Christ, the Christ of God, who was as strong and manly as He was meek and humble in heart. Remember, meekness is not weakness, and humility is not servility. It is true that the religion of Jesus Christ is exceptionally a woman's religion; it has lifted women to a significance never dreamed of before. But it is also as much a man's religion! Its appeal is for heroism, fearlessness, courage, self-sacrifice, and utter reality.

> **Remember, meekness is not weakness, and humility is not servility.**

His Unhesitating Acceptance of Torture and Agony

The manliness of our Lord Jesus was manifested in His unhesitating acceptance of torture and agony in order to save others from suffering and ruin, rather than yielding one iota of the truth. Our Lord Jesus could have escaped the cross if He had been willing to compromise with the religious rulers of the day who oppressed the masses. Yes, He could have escaped easily, but He would not. He pursued the path of absolute allegiance to God and His truth though the cross loomed black and threatening in the path. He did not deviate one step in order to avoid the cross.

If He had chosen to do so, when the emissaries of Annas,

Caiaphas, and the cowardly crowd who had conspired to bring about His death came to arrest Him in the garden, He could have escaped. If He had appealed to the Father, the Father would instantly have sent twelve legions of angels and delivered Him (Matthew 26:53). But He knew that if He escaped the cross, sinners would perish eternally.

On the Mount of Transfiguration, Jesus was transfigured in glory; He talked with Moses and Elijah of His death that He was about to accomplish at Jerusalem. He then turned His back on the glory, and once again He appeared in His incarnate body (Luke 9:31; Philippians 2:6-8). He descended the mountain and went to Jerusalem to die so that you and I might live.

And you and I must tread the same path if we choose to abide in Him, for it is written in God's Word: *He that saith he abideth in him ought himself also so to walk, even as he walked* (1 John 2:6). The path of manly, literal sacrifice of self to save others is the path He trod, and He has said, *If any man would come after me, let him deny himself, and take up his cross, and follow me* (Matthew 16:24).

Chapter 9

The Real Christ: His Peace, Joyfulness, and Optimism

Let all the house of Israel therefore know assuredly,
that God hath made him both Lord and Christ,
this Jesus whom ye crucified. (Acts 2:36)

I will greatly rejoice in Jehovah, my soul shall be
joyful in my God; for he hath clothed me with the
garments of salvation, he hath covered me with
the robe of righteousness, as a bridegroom decketh
himself with a garland, and as a bride adorneth
herself with her jewels. (Isaiah 61:10)

These things have I spoken unto you, that my joy
may be in you, and that your joy may be made full.
(John 15:11)

Peace I leave with you; my peace I give unto you:
not as the world giveth, give I unto you. Let not
your heart be troubled, neither let it be fearful.
(John 14:27)

He will not fail nor be discouraged, till he have set

justice in the earth; and the isles shall wait for his law. (Isaiah 42:4)

He that saith he abideth in him ought himself also so to walk, even as he walked. (1 John 2:6)

W e have already considered eight features in the picture which God has given us in His Word of His own Christ. The one we studied in the last chapter was in striking contrast, at first glance, and in apparent opposition to the three we had studied in the three chapters preceding it. In this chapter we shall study three features in the portrait together, because they are so closely related that it is almost impossible to separate them, though they really are distinct.

Jesus was always sure of Himself and of the happy outcome of whatever events occurred.

Furthermore, to be fully understood, they must be studied together. They are in some respects closely related to that feature we studied last, His manliness, but in other respects they are in striking contrast to it. Our subject in this chapter is the real Christ: His imperturbable peace, constant joyfulness, and unconquerable optimism.

His Imperturbable Peace

We shall consider first the imperturbable peace of the real Christ, the Christ of God's own endorsement, Christ Jesus. The whole life of our Lord was characterized by a calm composure, a self-possession, a divine serenity, and an abiding and abounding peace that nothing could disturb. He was always sure of Himself and of the happy outcome of whatever events occurred, no matter how disturbing they might appear to be.

Calm in the Midst of Peril

The imperturbable peace of the Christ of God was manifested by His perfect calm and confidence in an hour of apparently great peril. We see this in Mark: *And there ariseth a great storm of wind, and the waves beat into the boat, insomuch that the boat was now filling. And he himself was in the stern, asleep on the cushion: and they awake him, and say unto him, Teacher, carest thou not that we perish? And he awoke, and rebuked the wind, and said unto the sea, Peace, be still. And the wind ceased, and there was a great calm. And he said unto them, Why are ye fearful? have ye not yet faith?* (Mark 4:37-40; cf. Luke 8:22-25; Matthew 8:23-26).

We see from parallel accounts in Matthew and Luke that His disciples were almost beside themselves with fear. Our Lord Jesus was not only perfectly calm and fearless, He was also even surprised at their fearfulness and gently rebuked it, exclaiming, *Why are ye fearful? have ye not yet faith?* The great calm that lay on the bosom of the recent storm in Galilee was nothing compared to the great calm that possessed His own heart during all that wild and tempestuous scene.

Confidence in the Face of Calamity

The imperturbable peace of Christ Jesus was manifested in His calm confidence in the face of the crushing calamity and overwhelming sorrow of others whom He loved and wished to help. This is illustrated in the case of the death of the daughter of Jairus as recorded in Mark 5 and Luke 8. Mark's account is recorded in verses 35 to 42:

> *While he yet spake, they come from the ruler of the*

*synagogue's house, saying, Thy daughter is dead:
why troublest thou the Teacher any further? But
Jesus, not heeding the word spoken, saith unto the
ruler of the synagogue, Fear not, only believe. And
he suffered no man to follow with him, save Peter,
and James, and John the brother of James. And they
come to the house of the ruler of the synagogue; and
he beholdeth a tumult, and many weeping and wail-
ing greatly. And when he was entered in, he saith
unto them, Why make ye a tumult, and weep? the
child is not dead, but sleepeth. And they laughed
him to scorn. But he, having put them all forth,
taketh the father of the child and her mother and
them that were with him, and goeth in where the
child was. And taking the child by the hand, he saith
unto her, Talitha cumi; which is, being interpreted,
Damsel, I say unto thee, Arise. And straightway the
damsel rose up, and walked; for she was twelve years
old. And they were amazed straightway with a great
amazement.*

Notice the excitement, the tumult, and the excessive grief of
the others on the one hand and the perfect calm, peace, and
confidence of the Lord Jesus on the other hand.

Peace in the Face of Death
The imperturbable peace of the Christ of God was manifested
by His serene and exultant peace in expectation of His own
death, a death of unparalleled and inconceivable sorrow, shame,
and agony. His soul was *exceeding sorrowful, even unto death*
(Matthew 26:38). His heart was breaking with the weight of
man's reproach (Psalm 69:20), but underneath all the sorrow

and agony as the Sin-Bearer of the whole race was the deep, harmonious undertone of perfect peace.

For example, He said to His disciples who were crushed with the revelation of His coming death, *Let not your heart be troubled: believe in God, believe also in me* (John 14:1). We see it again in the twenty-seventh verse of the same chapter, where with a wondrous smile of perfect serenity, He gently whispered, *Peace I leave with you; my peace I give unto you: not as the world giveth, give I unto you. Let not your heart be troubled, neither let it be fearful.*

Perfect Rest on the Cross

The imperturbable peace of the Lord Jesus was manifested by His perfect rest in God even when, hanging on the cross, the iniquity of us all was laid upon Him, and the Father hid His face from Him because He was our Sin-Bearer. It is true that He cried with a breaking heart in unutterable mental and spiritual agony, *My God, my God, why hast thou forsaken me?* (Matthew 27:46), and then there came welling up from the deeper depths of His innermost spirit that other cry of perfect trust and peace: *Father, into thy hands I commend my spirit* (Luke 23:46). And as He uttered that last cry of perfect peace and hope and handed His spirit over to the Father, His earthly life ended in a glorious sunburst of peace triumphant to the very end.

In this peace that nothing can disturb, it is our privilege to follow Him.

In this peace that nothing can disturb, it is our privilege to follow Him. Whatever perils, losses, and agonies we may be called to face, we do not know. Whatever real persecutions and crosses we may be called to bear, no one can tell. When there is a loud call for sacrifice for others and the end rapidly draws near, we still know that they cannot possibly match the sorrow, agony, and shame He bore for us, and yet He said, *Peace I leave with you; my peace I give unto you: not as the world giveth, give I unto you. Let not your heart be troubled, neither let it be fearful* (John 14:7).

His Constant Joyfulness

Now let's look at another feature God has portrayed in His picture of the real Christ, His crucified Son: His constant joyfulness.

Isaiah tells us that the coming Christ of God was to be *a man of sorrows, and acquainted with grief* (Isaiah 53:3). He goes on to give us a detailed and vivid description of the appalling sorrows and griefs that would overtake the suffering Messiah as He made full atonement for our transgressions and iniquities. Later, after telling us all these griefs that the Messiah would suffer for us, he adds, *He shall see of the travail of his soul, and shall be satisfied* (Isaiah 53:11).

This is a figure taken from the terrible birth pangs of the mother, followed by that wondrous joy that only a mother can know as she looks into the face of her newborn babe, the most beautiful and entrancing sight her eyes have ever gazed upon. Our Lord uses the same figure in speaking to His disciples of the transporting joy that was to be theirs. After His resurrection, this joy would be the outcome of the heart-rending pangs they would experience at His crucifixion: *Ye shall weep and lament, but the world shall rejoice: ye shall be sorrowful, but your sorrow shall be turned into joy. A woman when she is in travail hath sorrow, because her hour is come: but when she is delivered of the child, she remembereth no more the anguish, for the joy that a man is born into the world. And ye therefore now have sorrow: but I will see you again, and your heart shall rejoice, and your joy no one taketh away from you* (John 16:20-22).

This is not all. On the night before His crucifixion, with

the cross and all its associated agonies fully in view, Jesus, our Lord and Christ, said to His disciples, *These things have I spoken unto you, that my joy may be in you, and that your joy may be made full* (John 15:11). He spoke of *my joy,* mind you, the joy that now fills and thrills His heart.

In substance, then, our Lord said, "When my joy, the joy that now fills and thrills my heart, shall be yours, your joy shall be full." The American Standard Version reads: *made full;* the English revisers translate it as *fulfilled.* Turn that word *fulfilled* around and you will understand what Jesus actually said: "filled full." When you get the joy that our Lord Jesus had even when contemplating His own crucifixion, your joy will be filled full – then and not until then. His joy was fullness of joy, joy filled to the brim. The *Man of Sorrows,* though He was our Sin-Bearer, He was, at the same time, the most joyous man that ever walked this earth.

What were the sources of His joy?

Obedience and Fruitfulness
The first source of His joy was that of obeying God and bearing fruit for Him. This appears in the verse just quoted. He says, *These things have I spoken unto you, that my joy may be in you, and that your joy may be made full.* What were the things He had just *spoken unto* them that He refers to here? Obedience and fruit-bearing. Note the verse immediately preceding this: *If ye keep my commandments, ye shall abide in my love; even as I have kept my Father's commandments, and abide in his love* (John 15:10). From these words, it is evident that His joy was in doing the Father's will.

The same thought comes out again in John 4:34: *My meat is to do the will of him that sent me, and to accomplish his work.* Now look at the other words He had just spoken in John 15:8: *Herein is my Father glorified, that ye bear much fruit; and so shall ye be my disciples.* His joy was the joy of bearing fruit for God. These two joys – the joy of obedience to God and the joy of bearing fruit for God – are two of the greatest joys possible to man, and they are both open to us also.

Salvation of Souls

The second source of the joy of Christ Jesus was closely connected with the first. It was the joy of saving souls. This is seen in one of our texts, in a prophetic preview of the coming Christ: *He shall see of the travail of his soul, and shall be satisfied* (Isaiah 53:11). The fruit of the travail of His soul, the pangs of spiritual birth which the Messiah would see and in which He would be satisfied and compensated for all He had suffered, would be the newborn souls that would result from His sufferings unto death. Our Lord feels more than compensated for all the agonies He has endured when He sees men born again and thus saved.

He exultantly cries to the assembled hosts of heaven: *Rejoice with me, for I have found my sheep which was lost* (Luke 15:6). There are few greater joys to a true heart than the joy of seeing others saved, and this joy too can be ours. It can be ours if we are willing to pay the price, and that price is anguish of soul.

Meditation on the Father's Will

The third source of Christ's joy was joy in the meditation on, or contemplation of, the Father's will. This appears in Luke 10:21: *In that same hour he rejoiced in the Holy Spirit, and said, I thank thee, O Father, Lord of heaven and earth, that thou didst hide these things from the wise and understanding, and didst reveal them unto babes: yea, Father; for so it was well-pleasing in thy sight.*

The word translated *rejoiced* in this passage is a peculiarly expressive word. It means "to exult" or "to rejoice exceedingly." It is translated *be exceeding glad* in Matthew 5:12, and *rejoice greatly* in 1 Peter 1:8, where it is accompanied by the very suggestive descriptive phrase: *with joy unspeakable and full of glory.* It may seem at first glance as if this joy were the same as that spoken of under our first heading, but they are really quite different. That was the joy of *doing* the Father's will; this is the joy of the *glad contemplating* of the Father's will in its wisdom and all its infinite excellence. This joy can also be and should be ours, and it is a very great joy.

God Himself

The fourth source of Christ's joy was God Himself. This appears in another prophetic picture of the coming of the Christ of God: *I will greatly rejoice in Jehovah, my soul shall be joyful in my God* (Isaiah 61:10). The picture is of the coming Messiah. Our Lord said that the opening verses of this same chapter referred to Himself (Luke 4:17-21; cf. Isaiah 61:1-2). This was the deepest source of Christ's joy, God Himself. Joy in God was His supreme joy. Joy in God is joy unchangeable and inexhaustible.

> **Joy in God is joy unchangeable and inexhaustible.**

This joy is open to us also, and when we know it, nothing can mar our joy, for however circumstances may change, God is always the same, and He is infinite; the joy that is rooted in Him partakes of His own infiniteness. Whether we hang on a cross or sit on a throne, our joy, if it is in the infinite God, will be *unspeakable and full of glory,* as our Lord's joy was. When at the age of ninety-five Polycarp was writhing in physical agony as he burned at the stake, he was at the same time moved with unutterable joy and shouted, "Welcome cross of Christ, welcome eternal life," because, like his Master's, his joy was in God.

His Unconquerable Optimism

Let us now look at one more feature of the Christ that God portrays in His Word – His unconquerable optimism. We shall see that our Lord Jesus was not only the world's greatest saint, greatest Savior, greatest teacher, and greatest Lord and Master, but He was also the world's greatest and sanest optimist. His optimism was not of the shallow kind, so common, boastful, and blatant today – the optimism that comes from closing one's eyes to clearly evident facts. His optimism was the optimism that comes by seeing – with the clear eye of faith in an infinitely wise, loving, and powerful God – the ultimate bearing of facts in the wise, loving, and far-seeing purpose of God.

We have a striking portrayal of the unconquerable optimism of the real Christ in another preview of the coming Messiah that was granted to Isaiah: *He will not fail nor be discouraged, till he have set justice in the earth; and the isles shall wait for his law* (Isaiah 42:4). There would indeed be much to discourage Him. He would find Himself opposed by all the ecclesiastical, political, and military forces of the day. He would be betrayed by one of His own chosen disciples and denied by another; every one of them would forsake Him and flee. He would be subjected to such losses, agonies, suffering, and shame as no other man ever endured on this earth. But in the face of it all, He would refuse to be in the least *discouraged,* knowing that God reigns, and He would at last *set justice in the earth* and that *the isles* would *wait for his law,* though it would take His own humiliating death to accomplish it. He saw the God-ward side and therefore the bright side of everything.

Bright Side of Persecution
The unconquerable optimism of the real Christ was manifested in His seeing the bright side of fierce persecution. This we see in Matthew: *Blessed are they that have been persecuted for*

righteousness' sake: for theirs is the kingdom of heaven. Blessed are ye when men shall reproach you, and persecute you, and say all manner of evil against you falsely, for my sake. Rejoice, and be exceeding glad: for great is your reward in heaven: for so persecuted they the prophets that were before you (Matthew 5:10-12).

To the average mind, harsh persecution does not seem a bright thing, but it did to the mind of Christ because He saw the God-ward side of it and the glorious outcome of it, and so should we.

We should not whine over our persecutions, but we should shout over them, even as the Lord Jesus commanded us:

> *Blessed are ye, when men shall hate you, and when they shall separate you from their company, and reproach you, and cast out your name as evil, for the Son of man's sake. Rejoice in that day, and leap for joy: for behold, your reward is great in heaven; for in the same manner did their fathers unto the prophets* (Luke 6:22-23).

> *The sufferings of this present time are not worthy to be compared with the glory which shall be revealed to us-ward* (Romans 8:18).

> *Our light affliction, which is for the moment, worketh for us more and more exceedingly an eternal weight of glory* (2 Corinthians 4:17).

> *If we suffer, we shall also reign with him* (2 Timothy 2:12).

> *If so be that we suffer with him, that we may be also glorified with him* (Romans 8:17).

The Outcome for Others

The unconquerable optimism of Christ Jesus manifested itself in His seeing the blessed outcome for others from His humiliating death. We see this in John 12:31-33: *Now is the judgment of this world: now shall the prince of this world be cast out. And I, if I be lifted up from the earth, will draw all men unto myself. But this he said, signifying by what manner of death he should die.*

Our Lord was facing the cross when He uttered these words. The cross was drawing very near. He saw clearly all the agony of the cross for Himself, but He saw something even more clearly, and upon that gloriously bright view of the cross, He fastened His whole attention. He saw the cross as the mighty magnet that would draw all races, kinds, and conditions of men to Himself. He saw the cross as the judgment of the prince of this world, as the end of Satan's power.

He saw that through His own death He would *bring to nought him that had the power of death, that is, the devil* (Hebrews 2:14). So, in whatever appalling sufferings we may be called upon to endure for Christ, we also ought to see the good for other men and the glory to God that is to come through our suffering. Then we can become optimistic even in a fiery furnace.

We see the same thing illustrated in our Lord's words: *Verily, verily, I say unto you, Except a grain of wheat fall into the earth and die, it abideth by itself alone; but if it die, it beareth much fruit* (John 12:24). Here again He bids us to follow Him. He goes on to say, *He that loveth his life loseth it; and he that hateth his life in this world shall keep it unto life eternal. If any man serve me, let him follow me; and where I am, there shall also my servant be: if any man serve me, him will the Father honor* (John 12:25-26).

Seeing the Blessing from His Death

In the third place, the unconquerable optimism of Jesus, the

Christ of God, manifested itself in His seeing the blessing to Himself that was to come from His death of agony. We see this in John 14:28, where He said to His disciples in view of His fast-approaching death, the thought of which had filled them with such dismay: *Ye heard how I said to you, I go away, and I come unto you. If ye loved me, ye would have rejoiced, because I go unto the Father.* In His death, as terrible as it was going to be, He simply saw the door through which He must pass to be with the eternal Father, the object of His eternal and infinite love.

In the same way at a later time, Paul regarded his own death, as terrible as it was going to be, as the greater good for him, for *to depart, and to be with Christ; [was] far better* (Philippians 1:23).

Glorious Resurrection

The unconquerable optimism of our Lord also manifested itself in His seeing His humiliating death swallowed up in glorious resurrection. This we see in several places; for example, in John 2:19: *Jesus answered and said unto them, Destroy this temple, and in three days I will raise it up.* We see it again in John 16:20-22, where our Lord said to His disciples on the night before His crucifixion: *Verily,*

> **In His death, Jesus simply saw the door through which He must pass to be with the eternal Father.**

verily, I say unto you, that ye shall weep and lament, but the world shall rejoice: ye shall be sorrowful, but your sorrow shall be turned into joy. A woman when she is in travail hath sorrow, because her hour is come: but when she is delivered of the child, she remembereth no more the anguish, for the joy that a man is born into the world. And ye therefore now have sorrow: but I will see you again, and your heart shall rejoice, and your joy no one taketh away from you.

The Right Hand of Power
In the fifth place, the unconquerable optimism of the Christ manifested itself when on trial for His life before Caiaphas, with the certainty of condemnation to death confronting Him, in His looking forward to the time when He would sit *at the right hand of Power, and [come] on the clouds of heaven.* We see this in Matthew 26:62-64: *And the high priest stood up, and said unto him, Answerest thou nothing? what is it which these witness against thee? But Jesus held his peace. And the high priest said unto him, I adjure thee by the living God, that thou tell us whether thou art the Christ, the Son of God. Jesus saith unto him, Thou hast said: nevertheless I say unto you, Henceforth ye shall see the Son of man sitting at the right hand of Power, and coming on the clouds of heaven.*

Recall the scene: They had arrested Him; they had struck Him (John 18:22); He knew they were soon to spit in His face, tear the beard from His face, scourge Him, and nail Him to the cross. But He looked beyond it all to the day when He would be seated at the right hand of God, and then when He would come back to this earth in God's own chariot *on the clouds of heaven* with all heaven's glorious armies following in His train. So we too should look beyond the present loss, suffering, and shame involved in true discipleship to the day when, having overcome, we shall sit down with Christ on His throne even as He overcame and sat down with His Father on His throne (Revelation 3:21).

> So we should look beyond the present loss, to the day when we shall sit down with Christ on His throne.

Looking to the Glad and Glorious Day
The unconquerable optimism of the true Christ, Christ Jesus, manifested itself in seeing all the turmoil, discord, chaos, anarchy, and desolation that are coming upon this world as the

logical and inevitable outcome of having rejected and crucified its rightful King. His optimism is also manifested in His
seeing the outcome of the prophecy and precursor of the glad
and glorious day of that King's return for the salvation of this
wrecked and ruined human society of ours, and its transforma-
tion into the fit and eternal abode of God. This appears in a very
striking way in Luke 21:25-28: *And there shall be signs in sun
and moon and stars; and upon the earth distress of nations, in
perplexity for the roaring of the sea and the billows; men fainting
for fear, and for expectation of the things which are coming on the
world: for the powers of the heavens shall be shaken. And then
shall they see the Son of man coming in a cloud with power and
great glory. But when these things begin to come to pass, look up,
and lift up your heads; because your redemption draweth nigh.*

So we, too, as the night of the present dispensation of this old
earth's history darkens, should have hearts that are becoming
more and more lighthearted with high hopes built on God's
sure word of prophecy.

Note again, *when these things begin to come to pass;* what
things? The things just described: *upon the earth distress of
nations, in perplexity for the roaring of the sea and the billows;
men fainting for fear, and for expectation of the things which
are coming on the world: for the powers of the heavens shall be
shaken.* These are the things that cause the hearts of thought-
ful statesmen to faint *for fear, and for expectation of the things
which are coming* upon human society. What shall we do then?
Hang our heads? No. Tremble? No. Get frightened? No. *Look up,
and lift up your heads; because your redemption draweth nigh.*

The world's golden age lies in the future, not in the past –
the near future, not the remote future. These prophesied things
that are happening today in Russia, Poland, Germany, Italy,
France, England, and America all shout aloud, *Your redemption draweth nigh.* We have waited long, but it is coming and

coming fast. These are great days in which we are living. Great, not because of men's boasting of big drives for money or the biggest thing the church has ever undertaken, which is a lie, an outrageous and infamous lie, but great because the trumpets of God's fast-accumulating providences proclaim, "The King cometh, God's King."

Chapter 10

The Real Christ: His Prayerfulness

Let all the house of Israel therefore know assuredly, that God hath made him both Lord and Christ, this Jesus whom ye crucified. (Acts 2:36)

Who in the days of his flesh, having offered up prayers and supplications with strong crying and tears unto him that was able to save him from death, and having been heard for his godly fear. (Hebrews 5:7)

And it came to pass in these days, that he went out into the mountain to pray; and he continued all night in prayer to God. (Luke 6:12)

And it came to pass about eight days after these sayings, that he took with him Peter and John and James, and went up into the mountain to pray. And as he was praying, the fashion of his countenance was altered, and his raiment became white and dazzling. (Luke 9:28-29)

And it came to pass, when he had sat down with them to meat, he took the bread, and blessed; and

*breaking it he gave to them. And their eyes were
opened, and they knew him; and he vanished out
of their sight.* (Luke 24:30-31)

*He that saith he abideth in him ought himself also
so to walk, even as he walked.* (1 John 2:6)

We have studied eleven marked characteristics of the
real Christ, the Christ of God's own appointment, the
Christ of actual fact as distinguished from the Christ of popu-
lar fancy and philosophical and mystical speculation. The real
Christ is the Christ whose coming and conduct God allowed
His chosen prophets of the Old Testament to see in anticipatory
vision, and whose actual life on earth God inspired historians
to record with marvelous accuracy and fullness in the aston-
ishingly brief but complete records found in the four Gospels.

**Christ Jesus was no
self-absorbed mystic.
He loved the society
of His fellow man.**

We have studied His holiness, His love
for God the Father, His love for men,
His love for souls, His compassion, His
meekness, His humility, His manliness,
His imperturbable peace, His constant
joyfulness, and His unconquerable opti-
mism. We have not dwelt upon His geniality, His sociability,
His friendliness, or His love for home life.

Just let me point out that Christ Jesus, the real Christ, was
no ascetic and no self-absorbed mystic. He loved the society of
His fellow man. He was a welcome guest at social and festive
gatherings. His first miracle, in which He *manifested forth his
glory,* was performed at a wedding feast and for the distinct
purpose of saving that joyous and festive occasion from ending
in embarrassment, disappointment, and gloom (John 2:1-11).

He returned many times to Bethany for the solace of congenial human companionship and the restful gladness of the pleasant joys of home life (John 11:5). Even on His last visit to Jerusalem, with the cross only six days ahead of Him, He was the willing guest at a feast His friends in Bethany made for Him (John 12:1-2).

And when He went to the garden of Gethsemane for its awful conflict and agonies, He longed for human companionship. He not only took the eleven to the garden, but He also took a chosen three into the deeper depths of its shadows to be with Him as He prayed more earnestly. His sweat was as great drops of blood falling down to the ground. He was a winsome Friend as well as a mighty Savior and absolute Lord of majestic men. Did He not say during His last hours: *Henceforth I call you not servants; . . . but I have called you friends* (John 15:15)?

As we look in this chapter at that wondrous picture of Him which God has given us in the Bible, I invite you to consider carefully and earnestly a characteristic that stands out more prominently than almost any other, which underlies all those already mentioned – His prayerfulness. I approach this subject with more hesitation than any other we have had, because it takes us into the holy of holies of His life, where we must take off our shoes and tread softly.

In the brief record found in the four Gospels of the wondrous life of our Lord here on earth, the words *pray* and *prayer* are used at least twenty-five times in connection with Him. The fact of His praying is mentioned in other instances in addition to those where these words are found. The life of Christ, as we have seen in the past nine chapters, had many marked characteristics, but nothing is more marked than His prayerfulness.

Some years ago Charles Sheldon wrote a book, *In His Steps: What Would Jesus Do,* that had an immense circulation in which he tried to picture what Jesus would do in various circumstances of life if He were on earth today. It was largely pure and entirely unwarranted imagination, but as the Lord Jesus *is the same yesterday and to-day, yea and for ever*, I know one thing that He would do if He were on earth today (Hebrews 13:8). I know one activity in which He would expend much time and a great deal of physical and mental energy – praying. I do not know how He would manage a newspaper; I do not think He would manage one at all. But I know He would pray, pray, pray. And the one who does not spend much time in prayer is not walking *in His steps* and is not like Him.

How the Prayerfulness of the Real Christ Was Manifested

Let us consider first how the prayerfulness of the real Christ, not the Christ of man's imagination but the Christ of undeniable historical fact, was manifested.

Prayer through the Night
First, the prayerfulness of the real Christ, the Christ of the Bible, the Christ of God's own Word, was manifested by His continuing all night in prayer to God. Luke tells us: *And it came to pass in these days, that he went out into the mountain to pray; and he continued all night in prayer to God* (Luke 6:12). On another occasion we see our Lord in prayer from about sunset until after three o'clock in the morning (Mark 6:45-48). This whole night of prayer followed a day of intense and wearying activity when He had been so busy that He could not eat and had taken His disciples apart to *rest a while* (Mark 6:31). But the necessary and desired rest had been immediately broken in upon by the multitude who outran Him, and the entire day had been spent in teaching and healing the sick and feeding

the multitude. That exhausting day was followed not by sleep, but by a night of prayer (Mark 6:35, 46).

There is often a better way to recuperate exhausted energies than by sleeping. Often when we are so tired we cannot sleep and we waste time tossing to and fro upon our beds, if we would arise and pour out our hearts to God, we would get far more rest and go back to bed quieted. We would realize what the psalmist said: *He giveth his beloved sleep* (Psalm 127:2). Of course, we must understand that not every night of our Lord's life was spent in prayer, but many nights were. Here, too, we might wisely follow Him.

Early Morning Prayer
The prayerfulness of Christ Jesus was also manifested in His rising before daybreak and going to a solitary place to pray. Mark tells how He went to a solitary place the morning after a busy day and evening. During the day He had taught in the synagogue at Capernaum and had healed a man possessed with an unclean spirit. Then He had gone to the house of Simon and Andrew and raised Simon's wife's mother from the sickbed where she *lay sick of a fever.* As the sun set, the people, hearing of the wondrous things He had done, came flocking to Simon's house from every quarter, bringing unto Him *all that were sick, and them that were possessed with demons.* In fact, *all the city was gathered together at the door. And he healed many that were sick with divers diseases, and cast out many demons.* But as exhausting as the day had been and as late as He had retired at night, long before daybreak He had risen and gone far out into a desert place where He would not be disturbed, and there He prayed (Mark 1:29-35).

Happy is the man who has learned this secret from the Lord

> **Happy is the man who has learned this secret from the Lord – to get alone with God in the early morning.**

– to get alone with God in the early morning while others are sleeping, that he may have undisturbed communion with God and ample time for prayer. If we would all do this, there would be more likeness to Christ in our character and conduct and more effectiveness in our service.

Years ago, I read about one of the most successful statesmen England has ever produced, the first Earl of Cairns. Before his death, he had said that if he had any success in life, he attributed it more to this fact than any other – for years he had given the first two hours of every day to the study of the Word of God and prayer.

When I was in England, I had the privilege of meeting the widow of Lord Cairns at dinner at Lord Kinnaird's house and of taking her to the banquet. After the dinner was over, I said to her, "Lady Cairns, I read some years ago that your husband said that if he had any success in life, he attributed it more to the fact that for years he had given the first two hours of every day to the study of the Word of God and prayer. Is that true?"

Lady Cairns replied, "I cannot say positively about the two hours, but I know that whatever hour of night we reached home from parliament – I always went with him, and we always rode home together – whether midnight, one, two, or three o'clock in the morning, he always rose at the same early hour in the morning. He shut himself up alone with his God and with his Bible." And she added, "When he was a member of Lord Disraeli's cabinet and there was a stormy session, when my husband entered, Disraeli would say, 'Now we will have peace; the Earl of Cairns has come.'"

Prayerful Preparation for Crises
The prayerfulness of Christ Jesus was manifested by His preparing for all the crises and great events of His life by prayer. In Luke we are told that it was as He was *praying, the heaven was*

opened, and the Holy Ghost descended in a bodily shape like a dove upon him, and a voice came from heaven, which said, Thou art my beloved Son; in thee I am well pleased (Luke 3:21-22). So we see He prayed before His baptism with the Spirit and His entrance into His public ministry. In Mark we see Him praying before entering upon an evangelistic tour (Mark 1:35-36). Later in Luke we see Him spending a night in prayer before choosing the twelve whom He would train to be the leaders in the early church (Luke 6:12-13). Luke also tells us that it was after a special season of prayer with His disciples that He announced to them His approaching death (Luke 9:18, 21-22). It is evident that He prepared for all the great crises of life by special seasons of intensive prayer. This is a lesson for us, a much-needed lesson.

Some years ago, thirty denominations in this country undertook what they affirmed as "the biggest thing the church of Christ has ever undertaken." They put many millions of dollars into the preliminary campaign to raise the money. They did more extensive advertising than the greatest business corporations in the world have ever ventured upon. And what were their prayer preparations for this mighty event? The Christians of the land were urged in thousands of newspaper advertisements to give only five minutes to secret prayer on the day the campaign was launched. It would be ludicrous, if it were not sad enough to almost break the heart of anyone who really knows the real Christ and the spirit and method of His life to not pray more than this.

Praying Alone after Achievements
The prayerfulness of the Christ of God was manifested by His retreating to pray alone after the great achievements of His life. We see this illustrated in Matthew: *And after he had sent the multitudes away, he went up into the mountain apart to pray:*

and when even was come, he was there alone (Matthew 14:23). This was at the close of a day filled with some of the most marvelous displays of divine compassion and divine power in His whole life. He had healed multitudes of the sick by His word or His touch and crowned it all by a display of divine creative power by feeding *five thousand men, besides women and children* with five small loaves and two small fishes (Matthew 14:19-21).

The multitudes were carried away with an enthusiasm for Him that knew no bounds. They wished to take Him and make Him king on the spot, but no, He wanted none of their applause and dismissed them. He dismissed the twelve also and then went into a secluded part of the mountain to pray, remaining there nine hours alone with God in prayer.

Why? First, that He might gather His strength. His miracles cost Him something – an expenditure and loss of power (Mark 5:30). But furthermore, He wanted to guard against temptations to pride, self-satisfaction, or contentment with the work already achieved. Let's never forget that our Lord Jesus, while He was very God of very God, was also a real man, subject to the same temptations that we are; and in order to set us an example, He met them with the same weapons that we must use: the Word of God and prayer.

If we would really pray after the great achievements of life, we might go on to greater ones.

What a lesson for us! With most of us, it is more common to pray before the great events of life than after them, but the latter is as important as the former. If we would really pray after the great achievements of life, we might go on to greater ones. But since we do not, we are either puffed up or exhausted by them, so we proceed to no greater achievements.

Withdrawing from Busyness to Pray
The prayerfulness of Christ Jesus was manifested by His

withdrawing from the multitude when life was unusually busy, and going into a solitary place to pray. For example, in Luke we read: *But so much the more went abroad the report concerning him: and great multitudes came together to hear, and to be healed of their infirmities. But he withdrew himself in the deserts, and prayed* (Luke 5:15-16). How unlike Him we are. We would have thought this to be the day of opportunity, the time to cultivate the crowd, the day to stay with them, the time to work and not to pray, as if praying were not the mightiest kind of working. But not so with our Lord. This was the time He needed to be alone with God.

Some men are so busy that they can find no time to pray, but apparently the busier Christ's life was, the more crowded with necessary activity, the more He prayed. There were times when He had no time to eat (Mark 3:20), and occasions when He had no time for needed rest and sleep (Mark 6:31, 33, 46), but He always took time to pray; the more the work crowded, the more He prayed. Many mighty men of God have learned this secret from Christ, but many other mighty men of God have lost their power because they did not learn this secret and have allowed increasing work to crowd out prayer. One of the mightiest men of God I ever knew lost much of his power in this way.

Preparing for Temptation through Prayer

The prayerfulness of Christ Jesus was manifested by His preparing for the temptation He saw approaching by prayer. We see a remarkable illustration of this in Luke: *And he came out, and went, as his custom was, unto the mount of Olives; and the disciples also followed him. And when he was at the place, he said unto them, Pray that ye enter not into temptation. And he was parted from them about a stone's cast; and he kneeled down and prayed* (Luke 22:39-41).

He prepared for the temptations He saw drawing near by prayer, so He was always victorious. The disciples, despite His solemn warning, slept while He prayed, so He stood and they fell. The calm majesty of His bearing amid the awful onslaughts of Pilate's judgment hall and of Calvary was the outcome of the prayer, the struggle, the agony, and the victory of Gethsemane.

Praying in the Midst of Ordinary Life

The prayerfulness of Jesus Christ was manifested in His praying in the midst of the most ordinary matters of everyday life. Our attention is repeatedly called to the fact that He prayed in connection with the most ordinary meal (for example, Matthew 14:19). Indeed, His manner of praying in connection with His everyday meals was characteristic of His behavior. When the disciples on the road to Emmaus had failed to discover who He was, though their hearts had burned within them while He spoke to them and opened the Scriptures to them, they knew Him instantly the moment He lifted His eyes to pray to God before breaking the bread (Luke 24:30-31). With most of us, it is for the little things that we most frequently forget to pray. Every step of Christ's life seems to have been accompanied and sanctified by prayer.

> **Every step of Christ's life seems to have been accompanied and sanctified by prayer.**

His Last Words

The prayerfulness of Jesus Christ was manifested by the last utterance of His earthly life being a prayer. This we see in Luke 23:46 where, as He breathes His last and gives up His spirit to God, He cries, *Father, into thy hands I commend my spirit.* And that was not the only prayer in those closing hours of His life spent on the cross, for He also prayed for the Father to forgive those who crucified Him (Luke 23:34). His life had been a life of prayer, and with a prayer it came to its fitting close.

Though our Lord Jesus undoubtedly was a lover of human society, nevertheless, in His deep sense of need for communion with God, we often see Him fleeing from the crowds to the solitary place (Mark 1:35) and to the hidden recesses of the mountains (Matthew 14:23) to pray. Each of the four Gospels makes mention of His going to the mountains to pray, and in Luke 22:39 it is added: *as his custom was.*

In his *Imago Christi,* Stalker has this suggestive comment: "When He arrived in a town, His first thought was which was the shortest way to the mountain, just as ordinary travelers inquire where the most noted sights are and which is the best hotel." He prayed alone by Himself (Matthew 14:23), with a chosen few (Luke 9:28), with the whole apostolic company (Luke 9:18), and in the midst of a great multitude (Matthew 14:19).

How Jesus Christ Prayed

We shall get no adequate picture of the prayer life of the Christ of God without giving some consideration to the question of how He prayed. The Bible has much to say about that.

With God's Glory in View

First, Christ Jesus prayed with God's glory first in view, that God might be glorified by answering the prayer. For example, note that marvelous prayer He offered in the presence of His disciples before His arrest, trial, and crucifixion. He began His prayer with these words: *Father, the hour is come; glorify thy Son, that the Son may glorify thee* (John 17:1). We see the same thing in the prayer He taught His disciples, which begins with these words: *Our Father which art in heaven, Hallowed be thy name* (Matthew 6:9).

In Submission

Second, Jesus Christ prayed in perfect submission to the Father's will. This we see in His cry of agony in the garden: *O my Father, if this cup may not pass away from me, except I drink it, thy will be done* (Matthew 26:42).

Standing, Kneeling, Lying

Third, as to the posture which He assumed in prayer, He sometimes prayed standing (John 11:41-42; 17:1), sometimes kneeling (Luke 22:41), and sometimes lying on His face before God (Matthew 26:39). If the sinless Son of God got down upon His knees, even upon His face before God, what attitude should we ordinary mortals assume as we go into God's presence?

With Intense Earnestness

Jesus prayed with intense earnestness. We see this in Luke where we read: *And being in an agony he prayed more earnestly; and his sweat became as it were great drops of blood falling down upon the ground* (Luke 22:44). The literal force of the word translated *earnestly* is "stretched-outedly." The idea is of the soul stretched out in the intensity of its desire toward God.

We see the same thing in Hebrews 5:7: *Who in the days of his flesh, having offered up prayers and supplications with strong crying and tears unto him that was able to save him from death, and having been heard for his godly fear.* The intense earnestness implied in these words comes out in two ways: first, in the words *prayers* and *supplications*. The word translated *prayers* is a strong and expressive word, meaning the definite expression of a definitely felt need; it means "entreaties."

The word translated *supplications* is found nowhere else in the New Testament. It is a peculiarly significant word and indicates "imploring supplications." But the intense earnestness of our Lord's prayer comes out still more clearly in the words *with strong crying and tears.*

The word here translated *crying* is a strong word meaning "outcry" or "clamor," the force of which is increased by the qualifying adjective *strong.* Literally translated, the words would read: He prayed with *mighty outcry.*

Some consider it an attainment of superior faith to always be very calm in prayer and "just take" in childlike confidence what they ask. Those who say this have either gone beyond their Master or do not know what Holy Spirit earnestness means. Not infrequently, their calm comes not from the Holy Spirit but from indifference. The Holy Spirit makes intercessions *with groanings which cannot be uttered* (Romans 8:26). In view of the example of our Lord, we need to be careful not to confuse the laziness of indifference with the "rest of faith." Any rest of faith that does not leave room for mighty conflicts in prayer and in action is not Christlike.

For a Long Time
Our Lord Jesus prayed with a large outlay of time. He spent whole nights in prayer. We have already referred to this in interpreting Luke 6:12. The time element in prayer is of great importance. By the use of modern machinery, a man can do more in a minute than he once could do in hours, **Effective praying demands time.** but no machinery has ever been invented nor can be invented by which the work of prayer can be expedited. Effective praying demands time, much time; and woe to the man whose accumulating activities lead him to curtail the time given to prayer.

With Repeated Requests
Jesus Christ prayed importunately; that is, He repeatedly asked for the same thing. We see this in Matthew 26:44 where the

Holy Spirit tells us: *He left them again, and went away, and prayed a third time, saying again the same words.* We see in the example of our Lord in this matter that it will not do to say that the failure to accept an answer after you ask the first time indicates a weakness of faith. It indicated no weakness of faith on the part of our Lord when in His intense earnestness and in the determination of faith, He uttered precisely the same petition a third time.

With Thanksgiving
Our Lord prayed with thanksgiving. In John we read: *So they took away the stone. And Jesus lifted up his eyes, and said, Father, I thank thee that thou heardest me. And I knew that thou hearest me always: but because of the multitude that standeth around I said it, that they may believe that thou didst send me* (John 11:41-42). In this case the thanksgiving was for an answer to prayer yet in the future and that could only be seen by the eye of faith.

With Faith
Our Lord prayed believingly, with the absolute certainty that He had received from God the petition that He asked of Him. We see this in the passage just quoted, where our Lord Jesus said, *I thank thee that thou heardest me,* though Lazarus still lay in the grave. His faith in God's answering His prayer was such that He thanked God for answering before the thing that He had asked was actually done. He believed; indeed He had no doubt; indeed He knew that the Father would grant His every request. We see John, the beloved disciple, following in the steps of His Master's faith in 1 John 3:22: *And whatsoever we ask we receive of him, because we keep his commandments and do the things that are pleasing in his sight.* And so we, too, should learn that when we approach God in prayer, resting on

His promise and asking something according to His will, we must believe that we have received (Mark 11:24).

What a striking contrast in the matter of prayer there is between the real Christ, Christ Jesus, and the Christ, the "Christ principle," of the so-called Christian Scientists. Mrs. Mary Baker Grover Patterson Eddy scoffed at the thought that there was a personal God who answered prayer. What Christian Scientists sometimes call prayer is not in any proper sense prayer at all. It is merely intense, concentrated, self-willed thinking, iterated and reiterated denial of the existence of the things from which they wish deliverance, whether it is sickness, pain, sin, death, or misfortune of any kind. "Demonstrating the truth," they sometimes called it, the devil-suggested substitute for prayer that had landed many in their graves and many others in divorce courts, including the founder; and many others ended up in the insane asylum.

I have a copy of *Science and Health* from a man who said Christian Science had robbed him of his wife and daughter and wrecked his home. In giving me the book, he said, "This has nearly landed me in the insane asylum." But the true Christ, the Christ of God, the Lord Jesus, really prayed, and by His prayers, He worked miracles, healed the sick, cast out demons, raised the dead, escaped death Himself, glorified God, and finished the work God gave Him to do.

We have come to the end of our studies of the wonderful picture of *the real Christ* that God has given us in His Word. Let's follow Him. Let's follow Him in His holiness. Let's follow Him in His love for the Father, His love for men, and His love for souls. Let's follow Him in His compassion, His meekness, His humility, and His robust manliness. Let's follow Him in His imperturbable peace, His constant joyfulness, and His unconquerable optimism. Above all, let's follow Him in His prayerfulness. That prayerfulness was in many ways the secret of all the other beauties and glories of that matchless life, that divine life, lived as a real man here on this earth under the same conditions that you and I live under. He lived with the same temptations and with the complete victory that can also be yours and mine.

And while we pray intensely, often in long vigils in the solitary place alone with God, let's never forget that closing prayer that God's Word teaches us, our prayer of response to the closing promise of God's Word: *Surely I come quickly. Amen. Even so, come, Lord Jesus* (Revelation 22:20). For when He comes, we shall be perfected in holiness, in love for the Father, in love for our fellow man, in love for souls, in compassion, in meekness, in humility, in manliness, in peace, in joy, in optimism, and in every grace and perfection and glory of Christ's character. For when He comes, *We shall be like him; for we shall see him even as he is* (1 John 3:2).

Reuben A. Torrey
– A Brief Biography

Reuben A. Torrey was an author, conference speaker, pastor, evangelist, Bible college dean, and more. Reuben Archer Torrey was born in Hoboken, New Jersey, on January 28, 1856. He graduated from Yale University in 1875 and from Yale Divinity School in 1878, when he became the pastor of a Congregational church in Garrettsville, Ohio. Torrey married Clara Smith in 1879, with whom he had five children.

In 1882, he went to Germany, where he studied at the universities at Leipsic and Erlangen. Upon returning to the United States, R. A. Torrey pastored in Minneapolis, as well as being in charge of the Congregational City Mission Society. In 1889, D. L. Moody called upon Torrey to lead his Chicago Evangelization Society, which later became the Moody Bible

Institute. Beginning in 1894, Torrey was also the pastor of the Chicago Avenue Church, which was later called the Moody Memorial Church. He was a chaplain with the YMCA during the Spanish-American War, and was also a chaplain during World War I.

Torrey traveled all over the world leading evangelistic tours, preaching to the unsaved. It is believed that more than 100,000 were saved under his preaching. In 1908, he helped start the Montrose Bible Conference in Pennsylvania, which continues today. He became dean of the Los Angeles Bible Institute (now BIOLA) in 1912, and was the pastor of the Church of the Open Door in Los Angeles from 1915-1924.

Torrey continued speaking all over the world and holding Bible conferences. He died in Asheville, North Carolina, on October 26, 1928.

Reuben A. Torrey was a very active evangelist and soul winner, speaking to people everywhere he went, in public and in private, about their souls, seeking to lead the lost to Jesus. He authored more than forty books, including *How to Bring Men to Christ, How to Pray, How to Study the Bible, How to Obtain Fullness of Power*, and *Why God Used D. L. Moody*, as well as editing the twelve-volume book about the fundamentals of the faith, titled *The Fundamentals*. He was also known as a man of prayer, and his teaching, preaching, writing, and his entire life proved that he walked closely with God.

Other Similar Titles

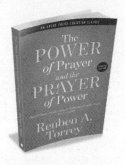

The Power of Prayer and the Prayer of Power,
by Reuben A Torrey

Prayer is the key that unlocks all the storehouses of God's infinite grace and power. All that God is, and all that God has, is at the disposal of prayer; but we must use the key. Prayer can do anything that God can do, and since God can do anything, prayer is omnipotent. No one can stand against the person who knows how to pray, who meets all the conditions of prevailing prayer, and who really prays, and if they are willing to pay the price. The price is prayer, much prayer, much real prayer, prayer in the Holy Spirit.

Available where books are sold.